Ketogenic Diet:
60 Delicious Slow Cooker
Recipes for Fast Weight Loss

Jeremy Stone

Elevate Publishing Limited

Table of Contents

Introduction

For years we were told that fats were bad for us and to be healthy we should eat more carbs. But with our knowledge of science and nutrition advanced, we now know fats aren't as bad as we once thought! This is where the Ketogenic Diet comes in. Scientific studies now show the dangers and risks associated with simple carb diets. At the same time, there are many studies that show the health benefits of a high fat, low-carb diet, including:

- **Increased Energy and Focus**

- **Increased Weight Loss**

- **Lowered Blood Sugar Levels**

- **Decrease in Hunger**

- **Lowered Bad Cholesterol Levels**

- **Reduction in Acne and Skin Inflammation**

Never Enough Time!

Time is the most valuable thing a man can spend.
-Theophrastus

Finding healthy and easy recipes is one of the biggest challenges you'll face when on a Ketogenic Diet. In our modern lives, we rarely have time to cook for ourselves every single day. Between work, bringing kids to practice, and cleaning up around the house, cooking healthy meals is usually the first thing to suffer. That is why it is important to have easy-to-make Keto-friendly recipes you can use when you are on the go!

All the recipes here take less than an hour of prep time. However, most recipes take only 15 minutes to make or less. Once the initial prep work is done, it's just a matter of set it and forget it. You can let your meal cook while you are at work or running errands. Then, when you come home, you have a delicious ketogenic meal to enjoy with your family!

The book is designed to make finding the perfect recipe easy. The book is divided into four parts: breakfast, lunch, dinner, and snacks. Under each section, recipes are organized from the quickest total time to make, to the longest. Each recipe includes full nutritional information, so there's no guessing how many carbs you're eating.

Thank you for choosing 60 Delicious Slow Cooker Recipes For Fast Weight Loss. If you have any questions or comments, I would love to hear them!

You can reach me by email at **elevatecan@gmail.com** or on Twitter at **@JeremyStoneEat**

Bonus: Ketogenic Diet – How A Nutritious, Low-Carb Diet Will Burn Fat Fast

As a special thank you to my readers, I am giving away free copies of my book Ketogenic Diet – How A Nutritious Low-Carb Diet Will Burn Fat Fast! Get over 30 quick and easy-to-make Keto recipes, designed specifically for busy people like you. You will get awesome recipes for breakfast, lunch, dinner, and snacks with full nutritional information.

To get instant access to this book and more awesome resources, check out the link below:

http://www.shortcuttoketosis.com/KetogenicGuide

As an added bonus, subscribers will be given a chance to get exclusive sneak peaks of upcoming books and a chance to get **free** copies with no strings attached. **Don't worry,** we treat your e-mail with the respect it deserves. You won't get any spammy emails!

A Quick Overview of the Ketogenic Diet

Have you ever wanted to have more energy in your day, feel better, and look better? Many people have found a way to achieve a better life with a simple diet. I know; it sounds too good to be true. Yet, it is really possible to gain more energy, feel better, and look better by changing the way you eat. There is no magic pill, rather, it is as simple as developing an eating plan that gives your body the nutrients it needs.

What is this magic eating plan? It is known as a Ketogenic Diet. This method of eating is not so new and has been around for thousands of years. Unfortunately, modern society is selecting convenience foods generally loaded with carbohydrates and refined sugars. Today, eating is often done on the run.

Convenience is what sells, and manufacturers satisfy consumers' demands. These convenience foods come with preservatives, dyes, added refined sugar, salts, and processed grains. While they may be convenient to our schedule, these foods are not convenient for our body to process.

The Ketogenic Diet may sound complex and technical; but simply put, this diet is feeding your body foods that it can process more easily. The human body is made to function using food for fuel, which in turn gives us energy. The Ketogenic Diet optimizes this process with the result of giving us more energy. There are four sources of fuel for the body: carbohydrates, fat, protein, and ketones.

But what are ketones? Ketones occur when fat in the body is broken down. The result of a Ketogenic Diet is that fat and ketones become the main source of fuel for the body. The key to eating a Ketogenic Diet is to consume more fats, some protein, and few carbohydrates. This allows the body to be in a state of nutritional ketosis.

Before starting any diet, you need to discuss the benefits/risks with your doctor. It is important to understand the impact a diet may have on your body and your medical conditions. This will help you choose a diet that will be safe and give optimal results.

Eating a Ketogenic Diet is not just eating a low carbohydrate diet. Rather than counting carbohydrates, consider being aware of your body and how it is responding to the foods you consume. Are you giving yourself the nutrients that you need? A Ketogenic Diet is a change in both lifestyle and mindset.

When the body uses carbohydrates to convert glucose to energy, blood sugar levels can drop fast. The results are hunger and cravings for sugar and carbohydrates. On a Ketogenic Diet, drops in blood sugar are minimized. This is because fats and ketones serve as fuel, rather than quick-burning carbohydrates.

Weight loss is hindered by foods that cause cravings for sugar, salt, and fats. These addictive foods cause over-consumption of food that never give a true feeling of satisfaction. Most often, processed foods are the culprits. On a Ketogenic Diet, these foods can be avoided and so are the resulting junk food cravings and hunger. Instead of calorie counting, stick to foods found in nature and that are simple to pronounce.

Foods such as grains, dairy, and refined sugar cause inflammation in the body. Inflammation hinders weight loss and causes toxins to build up in your body. After starting the Ketogenic Diet, the toxins will be removed and inflammation will decrease.

The above is an overview of the Ketogenic Diet. If you would like to learn more, I have a beginner's guide to the Ketogenic Diet where I go more in-depth with the mechanics of the diet and give you proven strategies to help you lose weight for good.

With *Shortcut To Ketosis: Lose Weight, Feel Great!* You will also learn...

- Awesome Shortcuts to enter Ketosis
- Over 100 Quick and Easy Recipes For All Meals – Breakfast, Lunch, Dinner, and Snacks
- Over 50 Full Colour Pictures
- Macro and Micro Nutritional Information For Each Recipe!

Get your copy at Amazon here:

http://www.shortcuttoketosis.com/LoseWeightFeelGreat

Benefits of a Slower Cooker

Time is precious; waste it wisely.

Having a good slow cooker to me is one of the must-have tools when you're on a Ketogenic Diet. Not only does it save time, but it makes cooking healthy meals incredibly easy! Here are some of the other many benefits of using a slow cooker:

More nutrient rich food – When foods are cooked normally, they lose many of their vitamins and minerals. However, when foods are cooked in crockpots, they retain much more of their vitamins and minerals. This is because food is cooked at a much lower heat for a longer time and high heat destroys nutrients. Also, more nutrients are captured with slow-cooked meals because the juices from the food are served with the meal.

Saves money – Slow cookers helps you save money in two ways. First, they use less energy than a stove or oven. Second, you can get away with buying less expensive cuts of meats. Slow-cooking even the toughest meat will soften it up if given enough time.

Less clean up – Since you're only using a slow cooker to make your food, the time you spend on cleaning up will be much less than with conventional methods.

Measurement Conversion Note

Some recipes in this book have ingredients that are given in metric units, and it's important to get the right amount of ingredients in your meal creations.

Here is a quick and easy measurement conversion breakdown:

8 Ounces (Metric) = 1 Cup (US)
1 Ounce (Metric) = 1/8 Cup (US)
1 Ounce (Metric) = 28.35 Grams

Slower Cook Do's and Don'ts

DO'S

Use the Right Size Slow Cooker —most recipes in this book work best using a 5 to 6-quart slow cooker. If you have a different size cooker, keep a close eye on cooking times and monitor the meal to make sure that the finished product is not overcooked.

Prep Your Slow Cooker – some recipes may call for prepping your slow cooker with cooking spray before cooking. If this is the case, overlook the simple steps. Otherwise this could end up being a mess to clean up afterwards.

Cook On Low – some recipes in this book will include options for cooking food on low or high, depending on your time schedule. It is recommended to keep heat on low to create the moistest, most tender dishes.

Follow Cooking Times – cooking chicken for longer than six hours at a time can leave it dry and stringy. Over-cooking beef can also make it tough and hard to chew. If you have to work all day and want to make a recipe that has a shorter cooking time, purchase a programmable slow cooker that switches to warm once cooking is complete. This will make each meal the best quality it can be, no matter how much time it takes.

Plan Ahead – one of the benefits of slow cooking is the amount of time it saves. To save time in the morning, prep the meat and vegetables the night before and store them in separate containers in the refrigerator. Then, in the morning, all you have to do is add the ingredients and set the slow cooker to the appropriate time.

DON'TS

Remove the Lid While Cooking – although sometimes it may be necessary to look inside your slow cooker to see its progress. Taking off the lid can affect the overall cooking time as it takes quite a bit of time to heat the slow cooker back up once the lid is removed. If you need to look inside the cooker, as a rule of thumb you should add an additional 30 to 40 minutes to the overall cooking time.

Overfill the Slow Cooker – slow cookers are usually designed to be filled at no more than two-thirds full. Keep this in mind when you're using your slow cooker, as it can greatly affect cooking times. Make sure to check your manufacturers' instructions before you start cooking.

Breakfast

Start your day off right with these easy-to-make breakfast ideas. Have a healthy meal ready to go first thing in the morning by preparing it the night before and setting it on a low temperature.

Cheesy Spinach Frittata

Prep Time: 15 minutes   **Cook Time:** Low for 1-1 1/2 hours

Slow Cooker: 1-quart

Serving Size: 354 g   **Serves:** 2-3

Calories: 564

Total Fat: 45.3 g **Saturated Fat:** 12.2 g; **Trans Fat:** 0 g

Protein: 32 g

Total Carbs: 11.7 g; **Dietary Fibre:** 2.1 g; **Sugars:** 5.3 g

Net Carbs: 9.6 g

Cholesterol: 277 mg; **Sodium:** 515 mg; **Potassium:** 529 mg

Vitamin A: 43%; **Vitamin C:** 61%; **Calcium:** 48%; **Iron:** 22%

Ingredients:
- [ ] 1 cup (packed) baby spinach, stems removed and chopped
- [ ] 1 cup mozzarella cheese (2%), shredded; divided into 3/4 and 1/4 cups
- [ ] 3 egg whites
- [ ] 3 eggs
- [ ] 1 Roma tomato; diced
- [ ] 4 tablespoons canola oil
- [ ] 1/2 cup onion, diced
- [ ] 1/4 teaspoon black pepper
- [ ] 1/4 teaspoon white pepper

☐ 2 tablespoons milk (1%)

To taste:
☐ Salt

Directions:
1. In a small skillet, heat the canola oil on medium heat. Add the onion and sauté for about 5 minutes or until tender.
2. Lightly grease the slow cooker with non-stick cooking spray.
3. In a large mixing bowl, combine the 3/4 cup mozzarella cheese, the sautéed onion, and the rest of the ingredients.
4. Sprinkle the remaining 1/4 cup mozzarella cheese over the mixture.
5. Cover and cook for 1 to 1 1/2 hours on low or until the eggs are set and a knife comes out clean when inserted in the center.

Eggs Florentine

Prep Time: 15 minutes   **Cook Time:** Low for 2 hours

Slow Cooker: 3 1/2 or 4-quart

Serving Size: 317 g   **Serves:** 4

Calories: 562

Total Fat: 47.9 g **Saturated Fat:** 27.7 g; **Trans Fat:** 0 g

Protein: 27.5 g

Total Carbs: 8.5 g; **Dietary Fibre:** 2.4 g; **Sugars:** 2.6 g

Net Carbs: 6.1 g

Cholesterol: 3487 mg; **Sodium:** 524 mg; **Potassium:** 784 mg

Vitamin A: 168%; **Vitamin C:** 38%; **Calcium:** 55%; **Iron:** 30%

Ingredients:

- 6 eggs, beaten
- 2 cups (225 g) cheddar cheese, shredded, divided into 2 portions 1 cup
- 1/4 cup (25 g) onion, chopped
- 1/2 teaspoon Italian seasoning
- 1/2 teaspoon garlic powder
- 1 teaspoon black pepper
- 1 package (280 g or 10 ounces) spinach, frozen, thawed, drained, chopped
- 1 cup (235 ml) heavy cream
- 1 can (225 g or 8 ounces) mushrooms, drained

Directions:

1. Grease the slow cooker with non-stick cooking spray. Spread the 1 cup cheese into the bottom. Layer the spinach, then the mushrooms, and the onion.

2. In a mixing bowl, combine the cream, egg, Italian seasoning, pepper, and the garlic powder. Pour the mix into the slow cooker. Top with the 1 cup cheese.

3. Cover the slow cooker with lid. Cook for 2 hours on high or until the center of the Eggs Florentine is set.

Breakfast Casserole

Prep Time: 20 minutes	**Cook Time:** High for 2-3 hours
Slow Cooker: 6-quart	
Serving Size: 150 g **Serves:** 8	
Calories: 343	
Total Fat: 28.5 g **Saturated Fat:** 10.9 g; **Trans Fat:** 0 g	
Protein: 17.2 g	
Total Carbs: 5.4 g; **Dietary Fibre:** 1.2 g; **Sugars:** 2.2 g	
Net Carbs: 4.2 g	
Cholesterol: 172 mg; **Sodium:** 835 mg; **Potassium:** 422 mg	
Vitamin A: 13%; **Vitamin C:** 30%; **Calcium:** 24%; **Iron:** 08%	

Ingredients:
- 6 eggs
- 6 bacon slices
- 5 ounces cremini mushrooms, finely diced
- 12 sausage links, cooked, cut into 1/4-inch rounds
- 10 ounces cauliflower florets, cut into bite-size pieces
- 1/4 teaspoon salt
- 1/4 tablespoon salt
- 1 package (8 ounces) sharp cheddar cheese
- 1 leek, cleaned, cut into 1/4-inch half-moon slices
- 5 tablespoons canola oil

Directions:
1. Grease the bottom of the slow cooker with non-stick cooking spray.
2. Put the cauliflower in a microwave-safe bowl. Sprinkle with the 1/4 tablespoon salt. Fill the bowl with enough water to cover the cauliflower. Place the bowl in the microwave and microwave for about 8 minutes.
3. Meanwhile, prepare the rest of the needed ingredients.

4. When the cauliflower is barely cooked, drain the water off. Put the cauliflower into the bottom of the slow cooker. Distribute the sausage pieces and the mushrooms over the cauliflower.
5. In a bowl, whisk the eggs and the 1/4 teaspoon salt together. Gently stir in the leeks. Gently stir 1/2 of the cheese into the egg mixture.
6. Pour the egg mixture evenly over the layer of vegetables and sausage in the slow cooker.
7. Cover with the lid. Cook for about 2-3 hours on high.
8. When cooked, sprinkle the remaining cheese over. Allow to melt for a few minutes. Slice and serve. Season with salt and pepper to taste.

Two Cheese Sausage and Pepper Casserole

Prep Time: 30 minutes	**Cook Time:** Low for 2 hours

Slow Cooker: 6-quart

Serving Size: 205 g   **Serves:** 10

Calories: 456

Total Fat: 35 g **Saturated Fat:** 13.5 g; **Trans Fat:** 0.2 g

Protein: 31.5 g

Total Carbs: 2.9 g; **Dietary Fibre:** 0 g; **Sugars:** 1.1 g

Net Carbs: 2.9 g

Cholesterol: 313 mg; **Sodium:** 875 mg; **Potassium:** 372 mg

Vitamin A: 13%; **Vitamin C:** 18%; **Calcium:** 23%; **Iron:** 13%

Ingredients:

- ☐ 24 ounces (2 packs 12-ounce) breakfast sausage, lean turkey
- ☐ 14 eggs, beaten
- ☐ 1 1/2 cups cottage cheese, rinsed and drained
- ☐ 1 green pepper, diced or cut into thin strips
- ☐ 1/2 cup green onions, sliced
- ☐ 1-2 teaspoons no salt all-purpose seasoning
- ☐ 2 cups grated cheese, cheddar
- ☐ 3 teaspoons canola oil, divided into 2 teaspoons and 1 teaspoon

To grease slow cooker:
- ☐ Cooking spray

To taste:
- ☐ Freshly ground black pepper

To sprinkle:
- ☐ 2 tablespoons green onions, sliced

Directions:

1. Grease the slow cooker with non-stick spray. Put the cottage cheese into a fine mesh colander. Rinse with cold water until the creamy part is rinsed away. Allow to drain well.
2. Meanwhile, in a large frying pan, heat 2 teaspoons canola oil and cook the sausages until well browned. When the sausages are cooked, transfer into a cutting board. Heat the remaining 1 teaspoon of canola oil. Cook the green pepper strips for about 2-3 minutes or until browned.
3. Cut the sausages into fourths. Layer the cut sausages into the slow cooker with the cooked green pepper strips.
4. Sprinkle the drained cottage cheese over the grated cheddar cheese. Season with no salt all-purpose seasoning.
5. In a bowl, beat the eggs well and then pour over the layered ingredients.
6. Cover and cook for 2 hours on low or until the eggs are firm and the cheese is melted.
7. Sprinkle with the green onions. Serve hot.

Mexican Breakfast

Prep Time: 20 minutes   **Cook Time:** Low for 5 hours; high for 2 1/2 hours

Slow Cooker: 4-quarts

Serving Size: 144 g   **Serves:** 10

Calories: 269

Total Fat: 21.2 g **Saturated Fat:** 7.6 g; **Trans Fat:** 0.1 g

Protein: 16.3 g

Total Carbs: 3.7 g; **Dietary Fibre:** 0.6 g; **Sugars:** 2.4 g

Net Carbs: 3.1 g

Cholesterol: 206 mg; **Sodium:** 615 mg; **Potassium:** 272 mg

Vitamin A: 10%; **Vitamin C:** 02%; **Calcium:** 15%; **Iron:** 09%

Ingredients:

- ☐ 1 cup cheese of choice
- ☐ 1 cup milk
- ☐ 1 cup salsa
- ☐ 1 teaspoon chili powder
- ☐ 1 teaspoon cumin
- ☐ 1/2 teaspoon coriander
- ☐ 1/2 teaspoon garlic powder
- ☐ 1/4 teaspoon pepper
- ☐ 1/4 teaspoon salt
- ☐ 10 eggs
- ☐ 12 ounces sausage
- ☐ 2 tablespoon canola oil, plus more

Toppings:

- ☐ Sour cream
- ☐ Avocado
- ☐ Salsa
- ☐ Cilantro

Directions:

1. In a large skillet, cook the sausages over medium heat until they are no longer pink.
2. Add in the salsa and the seasonings. Set aside. Allow to cool slightly.
3. In a large mixing bowl, whisk the milk and the eggs together.
4. Add in the cooked pork and the cheese. Stir well to combine.
5. Grease the bottom of the slow cooker with the canola oil.
6. Pour in the mix. Cover and cook for 2 1/2 hours on high or for 5 hours on low. Serve with toppings.

Roasted Red Pepper, Artichoke Hearts, and Feta Frittata

Prep Time: 20 minutes   **Cook Time:** High for 2 1/2 hours

Slow Cooker: 6-quart

Serving Size: 223 g   **Serves:** 6

Calories: 326

Total Fat: 26.9 g **Saturated Fat:** 7.1 g; **Trans Fat:** 0 g

Protein: 12.8 g

Total Carbs: 12.2 g; **Dietary Fibre:** 4.4 g; **Sugars:** 4.5 g

Net Carbs: 7.8 g

Cholesterol: 235mg; **Sodium:** 491 mg; **Potassium:** 444 mg

Vitamin A: 42%; **Vitamin C:** 176%; **Calcium:** 16%; **Iron:** 13%

Ingredients:

- ☐ 1 can (14 ounce) small artichoke hearts, drain and cut into small pieces
- ☐ 1 jar (12 ounce) roasted red peppers, drain and cut into small pieces
- ☐ 4 ounces Feta cheese, crumbled
- ☐ 8 eggs, beaten
- ☐ 1/4 cup green onions, sliced
- ☐ 1 teaspoon no salt all-purpose seasoning
- ☐ ½ cup canola oil

Optional: for garnish
- ☐ 2 tablespoons parsley

Directions:
1. Pour the artichoke hearts into a colander to drain. When well-drained, transfer to a cutting board. Cut into small quarter pieces. Put into the bottom of the slow cooker.

2. Pour the roasted red peppers into the colander to drain. Cut into about 1/2-inch squares. Put into the slow cooker. Add the green onions into the slow cooker.

3. In a bowl, beat the eggs until well-mixed. Pour over the vegetables in the slow cooker. Add the canola oil. Gently stir with a fork to distribute the ingredients. Sprinkle the crumbled feta over the top of the mix and season with the no salt all-purpose seasoning.

4. Cook for 2–3 hours on low or until the eggs are firm and the cheese is melted. While still in the slow cooker, cut into 6 portions. Serve hot. If desired, sprinkle with chopped parsley.

No Salt All-Purpose Seasoning

Prep Time: 5 minutes   **Cook Time:** 0 minutes

Serving Size: 22 g   **Serves:** 10

Calories: 62

Total Fat: 1.1 g **Saturated Fat:** 0 g; **Trans Fat:** 0 g

Protein: 2.4 g

Total Carbs: 13.1 g; **Dietary Fibre:** 3.6 g; **Sugars:** 3 g

Net Carbs: 9.6 g

Cholesterol: 0 mg; **Sodium:** 8 mg; **Potassium:** 209mg

Vitamin A: 12%; **Vitamin C:** 13%; **Calcium:** 11%; **Iron:** 21%

Ingredients:

- ☐ 1/4 teaspoon cayenne pepper
- ☐ 1 teaspoon onion powder
- ☐ 1 teaspoon ground mace
- ☐ 1 teaspoon ground black pepper
- ☐ 1 teaspoon dried sage
- ☐ 1 tablespoon garlic powder
- ☐ 1 1/4 teaspoons ground thyme
- ☐ 1 1/4 teaspoons dried savory
- ☐ 1 1/2 teaspoons dried parsley
- ☐ 1 1/2 teaspoons dried basil

Directions:

1. Mix all of the ingredients in a bowl. Store in a jar with seal.

Morning Meatloaf

Prep Time: 10 minutes	**Cook Time:** Low for 3 hours

Slow Cooker: 4-quarts

Serving Size: 294 g   **Serves**: 4

Calories: 720

Total Fat: 57 g **Saturated Fat:** 22 g; **Trans Fat:** 0 g

Protein: 44 g

Total Carbs: 6 g; **Dietary Fibre:** 2 g; **Sugars:** 2 g

Net Carbs: 4 g

Cholesterol: 270 mg; **Sodium:** 1340 mg; **Potassium:** 790 mg

Vitamin A: 25%; **Vitamin C**: 10%; **Calcium:** 8%; **Iron:** 20%

Ingredients:

- ☐ 1 onion, diced
- ☐ 1 tbsp. coconut oil
- ☐ 1 tbsp. fresh sage, minced
- ☐ 1 tbsp. smoked paprika
- ☐ 1 tsp. crushed red pepper flake
- ☐ 1 tsp. dried oregano
- ☐ 1 tsp. marjoram
- ☐ 1/4 cup almond flour
- ☐ 2 eggs
- ☐ 2 lb. ground pork
- ☐ 2 tsp. sea salt
- ☐ 3 garlic cloves, minced

Directions:

1. Heat the coconut oil in a skillet over medium-high heat. Add the onions; sauté until soft. Add the garlic; sauté for about 3 to 4 minutes, or until fragrant. Remove from the heat; set aside.
2. In a mixing bowl, combine the remaining ingredients. Add the sautéed onion and garlic. With your hands, blend the

ingredients well, making sure not to overmix. If you overmix, the meatloaf will become tough and mealy when cooked.

3. Transfer the meat loaf mixture into a slow cooker, shaping it into a meat loaf. Make sure that the sides of the loaf are not touching the slow cooker sides.

4. Cook for 3 hours on Low. Make sure not to let the loaf sit on warm. Otherwise, it will dry out.

5. Let the loaf cool for a bit, then cut into slices; store in an airtight container.

6. In the morning, heat a bit on oil in a skillet over medium high-heat. Add the meatloaves; cook until both sides are brown. Serve immediately.

Notes:
You can make the meatloaves on Sunday for a quick breakfast for about 7 days.

Egg and Sausage Casserole

Prep Time: 20 minutes	**Cook Time:** Low for 4-5 hours; high for 2-3 hours
Slow Cooker: 6-quarts	
Serving Size: 211 g **Serves**: 6-8	
Calories: 448	
Total Fat: 36.5 g **Saturated Fat:** 12.2 g; **Trans Fat:** 0.1 g	
Protein: 26.3 g	
Total Carbs: 4.3 g; **Dietary Fibre:** 1 g; **Sugars:** 1.3 g	
Net Carbs: 3.3 g	
Cholesterol: 341 mg; **Sodium:** 854 mg; **Potassium:** 417 mg	
Vitamin A: 16%; **Vitamin C**: 58%; **Calcium:** 15%; **Iron:** 14%	

Ingredients:

- ☐ 10 eggs
- ☐ 1 package (12-ounce) sausage, cooked and sliced
- ☐ 3/4 cup whipping cream
- ☐ 2 cloves garlic, minced
- ☐ 1/4 teaspoon pepper
- ☐ 1/2 teaspoon salt
- ☐ 1 medium head broccoli (about ½ pounds), chopped
- ☐ 1 cup cheddar, shredded, divided
- ☐ 3 tablespoon canola oil, or more, for greasing

Directions:

1. Grease the slow cooker well with the canola oil.
2. Layer half of the broccoli, half of the sausages, and then half of the cheese into the greased slow cooker. Repeat the layer with the remaining broccoli, sausages, and cheese.
3. In a large mixing bowl, whisk the whipping cream, eggs, garlic, salt, and pepper until well mixed. Pour over the layered ingredients in the slow cooker.

4. Cover and cook for 4–5 hours on low or 2–3 hours on high until the edges are browned and the center is set.

Eggs, Mushrooms, Cauliflower, Leeks, Cheese, and Sausage,

Prep Time: 15 minutes	**Cook Time:** High for2-3 hours

Slow Cooker: 6-quarts

Serving Size: 144 g   **Serves:** 8

Calories: 269

Total Fat: 21.2 g **Saturated Fat:** 7.6 g; **Trans Fat:** 0.1 g

Protein: 16.3 g

Total Carbs: 3.7 g; **Dietary Fibre:** 0.6 g; **Sugars:** 2.4 g

Net Carbs: 3.1 g

Cholesterol: 206 mg; **Sodium:** 615 mg; **Potassium:** 272 mg

Vitamin A: 10%; **Vitamin C:** 02%; **Calcium:** 15%; **Iron:** 09%

Ingredients:

- ☐ 6 eggs
- ☐ 5 ounces cremini mushrooms, finely diced
- ☐ 12 sausage links, fully cooked, cut into quarter-inch rounds
- ☐ 10 ounces cauliflower florets
- ☐ 1/4 teaspoon salt, plus 1/4 teaspoon salt
- ☐ 1 package (8 ounces) sharp cheddar cheese, Sargento, fine-cut
- ☐ 1 leek, clean, cut into quarter-inch half-moon slices
- ☐ Non-stick cooking spray
- ☐ Water

Directions:

1. Grease the bottom of the slow cooker with cooking spray.
2. In a microwavable bowl, add the cauliflower and 1/4 teaspoon salt. Pour enough water to cover the cauliflower; microwave for 8 minutes.
3. Meanwhile, prepare the sausages, mushrooms, and leeks.
4. When the cauliflower is microwaved, drain, and add to the bottom of the slow cooker.

5. Distribute the sausages and mushrooms uniformly over the cauliflower layer.
6. In a mixing bowl, whisk the eggs and the remaining 1/4 teaspoon salt, then stir in the leeks gently. Stir in half of the cheese in the egg mixture. Pour over the vegetable and sausage layer in the slow cooker.
7. Cook for about 2 to 3 hours on high, or until the eggs puff. Sprinkle the remaining cheese, let melt for a couple of minutes, slice while still in the cooker; serve. If desired, season with salt and then pepper to taste.

Cheesy Ham Scramble

Prep Time: 10 minutes	**Cook Time:** Low for 2 hours

Slow Cooker: 4-quarts

Serving Size: 150 g   **Serves:** 4-6

Calories: 250

Total Fat: 10 g **Saturated Fat:** 0 g; **Trans Fat:** 0 g

Protein: 15 g

Total Carbs: 3 g; **Dietary Fibre:** <1 g; **Sugars:** 2 g

Net Carbs: <3 g

Cholesterol: 300 mg; **Sodium:** 580 mg; **Potassium:** 210 mg

Vitamin A: 15%; **Vitamin C:** 2%; **Calcium:** 15%; **Iron:** 15%

Ingredients:
- [ ] 1 clove garlic, minced
- [ ] 1 teaspoon dried parsley
- [ ] 1/2 cup cheddar cheese, shredded
- [ ] 1/2 cup ham, cooked, chopped
- [ ] 1/2 stick butter
- [ ] 1/2 teaspoon oregano
- [ ] 6 large eggs
- [ ] 6 tablespoons coconut or almond milk
- [ ] Salt and pepper, to taste

Directions:
1. Heavily grease the slow cooker with the butter, leaving a little to melt in the bottom.
2. In a mixing bowl, , whisk all the ingredients together except for the ham. Stir in the ham and then pour the mixture into the slow cooker. Cook for 2 hours on low, stirring occasionally.

Egg Tuna Casserole

Prep Time: 30 minutes	**Cook Time:** High for 1 hour plus low for 2-3 hours

Slow Cooker: 3 1/2-4 quart

Serving Size: 280 g   **Serves:** 5

Calories: 4131

Total Fat: 24 g **Saturated Fat:** 11 g; **Trans Fat:** 0 g

Protein: 39.7 g

Total Carbs: 9.1 g; **Dietary Fibre:** 2.2 g; **Sugars:** 3.6 g

Net Carbs: 6.9g

Cholesterol: 257 mg; **Sodium:** 702mg; **Potassium:** 2597 mg

Vitamin A: 19%; **Vitamin C:** 23%; **Calcium:** 24%; **Iron:** 19%

Ingredients:

- ☐ 8 ounces (225 g) mushrooms, sliced
- ☐ 6 eggs
- ☐ 4 ounces (115 g) cheddar cheese, shredded
- ☐ 4 tablespoons (28 g) butter
- ☐ 1/4 teaspoon pepper
- ☐ 1/2 teaspoon salt
- ☐ 1/2 onion, chopped
- ☐ 1 cup (225 g) cottage cheese
- ☐ 1 cup (130 g) peas, frozen
- ☐ 1 can (340 g or 12 ounces) tuna, in water

Directions:

1. In a large skillet, sauté the onions and the mushrooms in the butter over medium heat. With the edge of the spatula, cut the mushrooms into smaller pieces while stirring. When the onion is translucent and the mushrooms soft, transfer into the slow cooker.
2. In a mixing bowl, whisk the eggs, cottage cheese, salt, and pepper together. Drain the canned tuna. Add into the egg mix.

Add in the peas. Pour in the egg mix into the slow cooker. Stir to combine. Sprinkle the cheddar cheese over the top of the mix.

3. Cover the slow cooker with the lid. Cook for 1 hour on high. Adjust heat to low and continue cooking for another 2–3 hours.

Spicy Beef Cabbage with Avocado Salsa

Prep Time: 45 minutes	**Cook Time:** Low for 6-8 hours, high for 3-4 hours
Slow Cooker: 3 1/2-quart	
Serving Size: 555 g **Serves:** 6	
Calories: 1093	
Total Fat: 84.2 g **Saturated Fat:** 29.2 g; **Trans Fat:** 0 g	
Protein: 63.8 g	
Total Carbs: 21 g; **Dietary Fibre:** 10 g; **Sugars:** 6.7 g	
Net Carbs: 11 g	
Cholesterol: 239 mg; **Sodium:** 470 mg; **Potassium:** 1258 mg	
Vitamin A: 12%; **Vitamin C:** 178%; **Calcium:** 13%; **Iron:** 50%	

Ingredients:
- ☐ 2 pounds beef chuck roast, well-trimmed, cut into thick strips
- ☐ 2 cans (4 ounces) diced green chilies with juice
- ☐ 2-3 teaspoons canola oil
- ☐ 1 tablespoon taco seasoning (or your favorite Southwestern spice blend)

For the cabbage slaw and dressing:
- ☐ 1/2 red cabbage, small head, cut into thin strips
- ☐ 1 green cabbage, small head, cut into thin strips
- ☐ 6 tablespoons mayo (or light mayo)
- ☐ 1/2 cup green onion, thinly sliced
- ☐ 2 teaspoons Green Tabasco Sauce, or more
- ☐ 4 teaspoons lime juice, fresh squeezed

For the avocado salsa:
- ☐ 2 large avocados, diced
- ☐ 1 tablespoon lime juice, fresh-squeezed
- ☐ 1 medium Poblano (or Pasilla) pepper, diced very small
- ☐ ½ cup cilantro, finely chopped (or green onion, thinly-sliced)
- ☐ 1 tablespoon extra-virgin canola oil

Directions:

1. Trim all the visible fat and any undesirable parts from the beef and then cut the meat into thick strips. (Save the trimmed parts for homemade beef stock).
2. Rub the beef strips with the taco seasoning.
3. In a heavy, large frying pan, heat the canola oil. When heated, brown the beef on every side.
4. Put the browned strips in the cooker. Pour the green chilies and the juice.
5. Cover and cook until the beef shreds apart easily.
6. When the beef is cooked, shred apart with 2 forks. Return it to the slow cooker to keep warm and absorb liquid while making the salsa and cabbage slaw.

For the cabbage slaw:

1. In a large mixing bowl, whisk the lime juice, mayo, and tabasco sauce. Test and adjust the tabasco to your preference.
2. Put the green onions and cabbage into the bowl and toss them with the dressing.

For the salsa:

1. Peel and cut the avocados. Put in a mixing bowl and toss with the lime juice.
2. Chop the cilantro finely.
3. Add the Poblano chili. Add the avocado. Drizzle with the canola oil.
4. Gently toss.

To assemble the bowl:

1. Put a layer of slaw.
2. Add a generous amount spicy beef.
3. Top with a couple of spoonfuls of salsa.
4. Serve with extra tabasco sauce, if desired.

Notes:

If making for less than 6 people, only dress the amount of cabbage you will need.

Refrigerate the ingredients individually. When ready to eat the leftovers, toss the cabbage and warm the beef.

Egg Chili Puff

Prep Time: 15 minutes	**Cook Time:** High for 2 hours plus low for 3 hours

Slow Cooker: 3 1/2-4 quart

Serving Size: 208 g   **Serves:** 8

Calories: 366

Total Fat: 24.8 g **Saturated Fat:** 13.6 g; **Trans Fat:** 0 g

Protein: 29.9 g

Total Carbs: 4.9 g; **Dietary Fibre:** 0 g; **Sugars:** 1.9 g

Net Carbs: 4.9 g

Cholesterol: 300 mg; **Sodium:** 1029 mg; **Potassium:** 190 mg

Vitamin A: 18%; **Vitamin C:** 14%; **Calcium:** 50%; **Iron:** 10%

Ingredients:

- 16 ounces (455 g) Monterey Jack cheese, shredded
- 12 eggs
- 2 cans (115 g or 4 ounces each) green chilies, diced
- 2 cups (450 g) cottage cheese, creamed
- 1 teaspoon salt
- 1/2 teaspoon pepper

Directions:

1. Grease the slow cooker with non-stick cooking spray. Turn the heat to high. While the slow cooker is heating, whisk all of the ingredients together in a mixing bowl.
2. Slowly pour the whisked ingredients into the slow cooker. Cover with lid. Cook for 2 hours on high. Adjust heat to low and continue cooking for another 3 hours.

Lemongrass Curry Drumsticks

Prep Time: 15 minutes	**Cook Time:** Low for 4-5 hours

Slow Cooker: 3-4 quarts
Serving Size: 110 g **Serves:** 5
Calories: 251
Total Fat: 19.9 g **Saturated Fat:** 15.4 g; **Trans Fat:** 0 g
Protein: 14.1 g
Total Carbs: 5.5 g; **Dietary Fibre:** 1.2 g; **Sugars:** 1.8 g
Net Carbs: 4.3 g
Cholesterol: 38 mg; **Sodium:** 637 mg; **Potassium:** 263 mg
Vitamin A: 1%; **Vitamin C:** 5%; **Calcium:** 3%; **Iron:** 9%

Ingredients:

- ☐ 10 drumsticks, skins removed
- ☐ 1 cup coconut milk (plus 1/4 cup, optional)
- ☐ 1 fresh lemongrass, thick stalk, rough bottom and papery outer skins removed, trimmed to the bottom 5 inches
- ☐ 1 large onion, thinly sliced
- ☐ 1 teaspoon five spice powder
- ☐ 1 thumb-size piece ginger, micro planed
- ☐ 1/4 cup fresh scallions, chopped
- ☐ 2 tablespoons Red Boat fish sauce
- ☐ 3 tablespoons coconut aminos or tamari
- ☐ 4 cloves garlic, minced
- ☐ 1/2 cup coconut oil
- ☐ Freshly ground black pepper
- ☐ Kosher salt

Directions:

1. In a large mixing bowl, put the drumsticks. Season with salt and pepper.
2. Put the garlic, lemon grass, ginger, coconut milk, coconut oil, coconut aminos, fish sauce, and 5-spice powder in a high-

powered blender. Blend until it turns to smooth consistency. Pour over the chicken. Mix well.

3. Put the onion into the bottom of the cooker. Put the drumsticks and the marinade on top.
4. Cover and cook for about 4-5 hours on low.
5. Serve with a sprinkle of chopped fresh scallions.

For extra creamy sauce:
When the stew is cooked, remove the chicken. Pour the sauce and the onions in a blender. Puree and then add 1/4 cup coconut milk. Blend again for a couple of seconds. Return the chicken and the sauce into the cooker. Set on keep warm.

Notes:
This will make a great make-ahead meal. When the dish is cooked, allow to cool. Store in a container and keep chilled in the fridge for a couple of days. To reheat, put in a pot and bring to a simmer. Adjust seasoning and serve.

Reminders:
Do not cook on high. Also, do not cook for more than 5 hours.

Sausage Balsamic Chicken

Prep Time: 20 minutes	**Cook Time:** Low for 7 hours, high for 5 hours

Slow Cooker: 3-4 quarts

Serving Size: 304 g   **Serves:** 14

Calories: 592

Total Fat: 45.6 g; **Saturated Fat:** 13.3 g; **Trans Fat:** 0.3 g

Protein: 38.4 g

Total Carbs: 5.4 g; **Dietary Fibre:** 1.4 g; **Sugars:** 3.3 g

Net Carbs: 4 g

Cholesterol: 141 mg; **Sodium:** 1409 mg; **Potassium:** 725 mg

Vitamin A: 13%; **Vitamin C:** 20%; **Calcium:** 4%; **Iron:** 15%

Ingredients:
For the chicken layer:
- ☐ 4 chicken breasts, boneless, skinless
- ☐ 1 teaspoon Italian seasoning
- ☐ 1 teaspoon garlic powder
- ☐ 1 teaspoon kosher salt
- ☐ 1/2 cup extra-virgin canola oil

For the sausage layer:
- ☐ 6 Italian sausage links (sweet, spicy or a combo), raw or uncooked
- ☐ 2 cans (14 1/2 ounces) diced tomatoes, organic
- ☐ 1 can (15 ounces) tomato sauce
- ☐ 1 cup water or chicken stock
- ☐ 1 teaspoon Italian seasoning
- ☐ 1 white onion, thinly sliced
- ☐ 1/2 cup balsamic vinegar
- ☐ 1/2 teaspoon garlic powder
- ☐ 1/2 teaspoon kosher salt
- ☐ 4-6 cloves garlic, chopped

Directions:

1. Put the chicken breasts into the bottom of the cooker. Drizzle with a couple of tablespoons of canola oil.
2. Add the salt, garlic powder, and the Italian seasoning directly onto the chicken. Don't mix. Just leave the seasoning on top of the chicken.
3. Lay the sausages on top of the seasoned chicken.
4. Lay the onion and the garlic on top of the sausage links.
5. Pour the tomato sauce, diced tomatoes, balsamic vinegar, and stock/water into the cooker.
6. Top with the remaining seasonings. Again, don't mix.
7. Cover and cook for about 5 hours on high or for about 7 hours on low.
8. Serve with spaghetti squash topped with flat-leaf parsley or fresh basil.

For the spaghetti squash:

Slice spaghetti squash lengthwise in halves. Scoop out the guts and roast with the meat side down at 400F for about 30–40 minutes. When roasted, turn over to cool slightly. With a fork, harvest the strands. Spoon the Sausage and Balsamic Chicken over. Top with flat-leaf parsley or fresh basil.

Greek Eggs Mix

Prep Time: 10 minutes	**Cook Time:** Low for4-6 hours

Slow Cooker: 3 quarts

Serving Size: 173 g   **Serves:** 6

Calories: 264

Total Fat: 21.3 g **Saturated Fat:** 6.2 g; **Trans Fat:** 0 g

Protein: 14.5 g

Total Carbs: 5.4 g; **Dietary Fibre:** 0.8 g; **Sugars:** 3.3 g

Net Carbs: 4.6 g

Cholesterol: 340 mg; **Sodium:** 476 mg; **Potassium:** 319 mg

Vitamin A: 31%; **Vitamin C:** 9%; **Calcium:** 15%; **Iron:** 12%

Ingredients:
- 2 cups spinach
- 12 eggs, beaten
- 1/2 tsp salt
- 1/2 cup tomatoes, sun-dried
- 1/2 cup milk
- 1/2 cup feta cheese
- 1 teaspoon garlic powder
- 1 teaspoon black pepper, grounded
- 1 tablespoon red onion powder
- 1 cup baby bella mushrooms, sliced
- 4 tablespoon canola oil

Directions:
1. Grease the bottom of the slow cooker with the canola oil.
2. In a large mixing bowl, whisk the milk eggs, salt, and pepper together.
3. Add the red onion and garlic powder. Stir to combine.
4. Add tomatoes, spinach, and mushrooms. Stir to combine.
5. Pour the mixture in the slow cooker. Cook for 4–6 hours on low.

Chili Chicken

Prep Time: 5 minutes	**Cook Time:** Low for 6-8 hours, high for 4-6hours, plus 7 minutes

Slow Cooker: 4-quarts

Serving Size: 217 g **Serves:** 12

Calories: 264

Total Fat: 12.1 g **Saturated Fat:** 2.2 g; **Trans Fat:** 0g

Protein: 32.6 g

Total Carbs: 6.2 g; **Dietary Fibre:** 2 g; **Sugars:** 3.2 g

Net Carbs: 4.2 g

Cholesterol: 83 mg; **Sodium:** 310 mg; **Potassium:** 470 mg

Vitamin A: 25%; **Vitamin C:** 41%; **Calcium:** 3%; **Iron:** 8%

Ingredients:
- ☐ 1 can (16 ounces) Italian tomatoes, diced
- ☐ 1 jar (16 ounces) salsa
- ☐ 1 large red pepper, chopped
- ☐ 1 medium yellow onion, chopped
- ☐ 12 chicken thighs, boneless, skinless
- ☐ 2 tablespoons chili powder
- ☐ 1/2 cup canola oil

Directions:
1. Grease the bottom of the skillet with the canola oil.
2. Chop the chicken thighs into 1-inch cuts. Put them into the cooker.
3. Pour the chili powder into the cooker. Stir well to coat the chicken cuts.
4. Add the vegetables and then stir.
5. Pour the salsa and tomatoes. Stir to mix.
6. Close the lid of the cooker and cook.
7. Serve with a dollop of guacamole wrapped in lettuce leaves or over cauliflower rice.

Notes:

This dish tastes better when cooked longer. You can also serve this with a sprinkle of shredded cheese. If you are not strict on your diet, you can add a handful of black beans or frozen corn before cooking.

Chicken Cacciatore

Prep Time: 15 minutes	**Cook Time:** Low for 4-6 hours

Slow Cooker: 4-quarts

Serving Size: 268 g **Serves**: 12

Calories: 279

Total Fat: 10.6 g **Saturated Fat**: 3.6 g; **Trans Fat**: 0 g

Protein: 35.5 g

Total Carbs: 7.4 g; **Dietary Fibre**: 1.5 g; **Sugars**: 3.6 g

Net Carbs: 5.9 g

Cholesterol: 106 mg; **Sodium**: 156 mg; **Potassium**: 794 mg

Vitamin A: 11%; **Vitamin C**: 13%; **Calcium**: 5%; **Iron**: 12%

Ingredients:

- ☐ 3 pounds chicken thighs or breasts, boneless skinless
- ☐ 2-3 cloves garlic, minced (or more)
- ☐ 2 tablespoons butter (or any oil of choice)
- ☐ 2 pounds cremini mushrooms (or white), halved if small, quartered if large
- ☐ 1/4 teaspoon red pepper flakes (less or more, depending on how spicy you want)
- ☐ 1/4 cup tomato paste
- ☐ 1/2 cup red wine
- ☐ 1/2 cup chicken stock
- ☐ 1 large onion, minced
- ☐ 1 can (16 ounces) diced tomatoes, drained
- ☐ 1 1/2 teaspoons dried oregano
- ☐ Salt and pepper, to season

Directions:

1. In a small saucepan, cook the onions, tomato paste, butter, garlic, oregano, and red pepper flakes until the onions are soft.
2. Put the onion mixture into the cooker.
3. Stir in the chicken stock, tomatoes, wine, and mushrooms.

4. Season the chicken with salt and pepper. Add to the cooker, mix everything to combine, and cook.
5. Serve over cauliflower rice.

Notes:
For a thicker sauce, precook, cover, and refrigerate overnight. When ready to serve, reheat and simmer until the liquid is reduced to thick consistency.

Chicken Musakhan

Prep Time: 15 minutes   **Cook Time:** Low for 6 hours

Slow Cooker: 3-4-quarts

Serving Size: 146 g   **Serves:** 10

Calories: 289

Total Fat: 15.2 g **Saturated Fat:** 2.9 g; **Trans Fat:** 0 g

Protein: 34 g

Total Carbs: 3.2 g; **Dietary Fibre:** 0.9 g; **Sugars:** 1.2 g

Net Carbs: 2.3 g

Cholesterol: 101 mg; **Sodium:** 99 mg; **Potassium:** 352 mg

Vitamin A: 1%; **Vitamin C:** 4%; **Calcium:** 3%; **Iron:** 10%

Ingredients:
- ☐ 2 1/2 pounds chicken thighs, boneless, skinless
- ☐ 1 1/2 tablespoons canola oil
- ☐ 1 teaspoon cinnamon (I used 1/2 teaspoon Vietnamese cinnamon)
- ☐ 1/2 ounce ground sumac (lemon pepper seasoning, lemon zest with salt, or lemon juice)
- ☐ 1/4 teaspoon ground allspice
- ☐ 1/4 teaspoon ground cloves
- ☐ 2 onions, halved lengthwise, thinly sliced
- ☐ Big pinch saffron (optional, but nice)
- ☐ Handful pine nuts
- ☐ Salt and pepper, to taste

Directions:
1. In a large microwave-safe bowl, combine the canola oil, onions, cinnamon, sumac, cloves, allspice, and saffron. Microwave for 2 1/2 minutes, stir, and then microwave for another 2 1/2 minutes.
2. Put the chicken into the cooker. Liberally season with salt and pepper.

3. Add the canola oil mixture. Stir to mix, nestling the chicken on the onions.
4. Cover and cook for about 6 hours on low or until done.
5. When ready to serve, sauté the pine nuts in a little canola oil over medium high until browned.
6. Finely chop the mint.
7. Season with salt and pepper.
8. Serve topped with pine nuts and mint.

Jambalaya Soup

Prep Time: 20 minutes	**Cook Time:** Low for 6 hours

Slow Cooker: 3-4-quarts

Serving Size: 325 g   **Serves:** 10

Calories: 371

Total Fat: 30.2 g **Saturated Fat:** 6.3 g; **Trans Fat:** 0 g

Protein: 19.8 g

Total Carbs: 7.5 g; **Dietary Fibre:** 1.6 g; **Sugars:** 3.1g

Net Carbs: 5.9 g

Cholesterol: 93 mg; **Sodium:** 1064 mg; **Potassium:** 344 mg

Vitamin A: 8%; **Vitamin C:** 39%; **Calcium:** 3%; **Iron:** 6%

Ingredients:

- ☐ 4 ounces chicken, diced
- ☐ 1 package (about12 ounces) spicy Andouille sausage
- ☐ 1 pound large shrimp, raw, deveined
- ☐ 1/2-1 head cauliflower
- ☐ 1 large can diced tomatoes, organic, drained
- ☐ 1 large onion, chopped
- ☐ 1/4 cup Frank's Red Hot sauce (or any hot sauce)
- ☐ 2 bay leafs
- ☐ 2 c. okra (optional)
- ☐ 2 cloves garlic, diced
- ☐ 3 tablespoon Cajun seasoning (or make your own below)
- ☐ 4 peppers (any color), chopped
- ☐ 5 cups chicken stock
- ☐ 1 cup canola oil

Homemade Cajun Seasoning: makes about 2/3 cups

- ☐ 2 tablespoons salt
- ☐ 2 tablespoons garlic powder
- ☐ 2 1/2 tablespoons paprika
- ☐ 1 tablespoon onion powder

- ☐ 1 tablespoon dried thyme
- ☐ 1 tablespoon dried oregano
- ☐ 1 tablespoon cayenne pepper
- ☐ 1 tablespoon black pepper

Directions:
1. Put the chicken, chicken stock, onions, peppers, garlic, hot sauce, canola oil, Cajun seasoning, and bay leaves in the cooker.
2. Cover and cook for 6 hours on low.
3. About 30 minutes before the 6 hours is up, add the sausages.
4. Meanwhile, pulse the cauliflower in a food processor until rice-like in consistency.
5. About 20 minutes before the 6 hours is up, add the cauli-rice and the shrimp.

Notes:
If you don't want to add the cauliflower rice in the cooker, steam it in the microwave. Serve topped with the jambalaya.

Chocolatey Chicken Mix

Prep Time: 30 minutes   **Cook Time:** Low for 4 to 6 hours

Slow Cooker: 3-4-quarts

Serving Size: 281 g   **Serves:** 8

Calories: 514

Total Fat: 36 g **Saturated Fat:** 6.8 g; **Trans Fat:** 0 g

Protein: 36.5g

Total Carbs: 13.2 g; **Dietary Fibre:** 2.4 g; **Sugars:** 8.1 g

Net Carbs: 10.8 g

Cholesterol: 89 mg; **Sodium:** 321 mg; **Potassium:** 600 mg

Vitamin A: 21%; **Vitamin C:** 27%; **Calcium:** 7%; **Iron:** 12%

Ingredients:
- ☐ 2 pounds chicken (legs and breasts) skinned, bone in
- ☐ 2 1/2 ounces dark chocolate (70% or above)
- ☐ 6-7 whole tomatoes, peeled, seeded, chopped
- ☐ 5 dried New Mexico chili peppers, rehydrated and chopped
- ☐ 4 cloves garlic, minced or crushed
- ☐ 1/2 cup canola oil
- ☐ 1/4 cup almond butter
- ☐ 1/2 teaspoon chili powder
- ☐ 1/2 teaspoon cinnamon powder
- ☐ 1 teaspoon sea salt
- ☐ 1 teaspoon cumin powder
- ☐ 1 medium onion, chopped
- ☐ Salt and pepper, to taste

For topping:
- ☐ avocado, jalapeno, and cilantro, all chopped

Directions:

1. Generously season the chicken with salt and pepper.
2. Put a pan over medium heat. Put the ghee in and warm. When ghee is warm, add the chicken and brown every side. Do this in batches when needed.
3. Put the browned the chicken in the cooker.
4. In the same pan, sauté the onion until it's translucent. Add the garlic and sauté for about 1-2 minutes. Transfer to the cooker.
5. Add the remaining ingredients into the cooker. Cover and cook for about 4-6 hours on low or until chicken is tender and pulls apart easily.
6. Serve topped with avocado, jalapeno, and cilantro.

Cajun Grits

Prep Time: 5 minutes	**Cook Time:** Low for 7 hours

Slow Cooker: 1-quart

Serving Size: 275 g **Serves**: 8

Calories: 283

Total Fat: 23.4 g **Saturated Fat**: 14.7 g; **Trans Fat**: 0 g

Protein: 11.6 g

Total Carbs: 6.8 g; **Dietary Fibre**: 0.8 g; **Sugars:** 2 g

Net Carbs: 6 g

Cholesterol: 71 mg; **Sodium:** 976 mg; **Potassium**: 70 mg

Vitamin A: 14%; **Vitamin C**: 0%; **Calcium**: 33%; **Iron**: 3%

Ingredients:

- ☐ 1 1/2 cups stone-ground grits
- ☐ 12 ounces grated cheddar cheese + more
- ☐ 2 cups cream
- ☐ 2 teaspoons salt
- ☐ 4 tablespoons of butter
- ☐ 6 cups water

Directions:

1. Grease the slow cooker with non-stick cooking spray.
2. Add in the water, salt, and grits.
3. Cook for 7 hours or overnight on low.
4. Before serving, remove lid. Add the butter, cream, and the grated cheese.
5. Serve with additional grated cheese or butter.

Cauliflower Hash Browns

Prep Time: 20 minutes	**Cook Time:** Low for 5-7 hours

Slow Cooker: 6-quarts

Serving Size: 156 g   **Serves**: 10-12

Calories: 328

Total Fat: 26.8 g **Saturated Fat:** 10 g; **Trans Fat:** 0.1 g

Protein: 18.8 g

Total Carbs: 3.5 g; **Dietary Fibre:** 0.9 g; **Sugars:** 2 g

Net Carbs: 2.6 g

Cholesterol: 245 mg; **Sodium:** 674 mg; **Potassium:** 276 mg

Vitamin A: 10%; **Vitamin C:** 22%; **Calcium:** 22%; **Iron:** 8%

Ingredients:

- ☐ 8 ounces (about 2 cups) cheddar cheese, crumbled
- ☐ 2 packages (5 ounces each) sausage, cooked and crumbled
- ☐ 12 eggs
- ☐ 1/2 teaspoon pepper
- ☐ 1/2 teaspoon dry mustard
- ☐ 1/2 cup milk
- ☐ 1 teaspoon kosher salt
- ☐ 1 small onion, diced
- ☐ 1 head cauliflower, shredded
- ☐ 4 tablespoons canola oil

To taste:
- ☐ Salt & Pepper

Directions:
1. Grease the slow cooker with the canola oil.
2. In a bowl, lightly whisk the milk, eggs, dry mustard, salt, and pepper.

3. Place 1/3 of the shredded cauliflower in the bottom of the slow cooker. Spread to even the layer.
4. Top with 1/3 of the onion. Season with salt and pepper. Top with 1/3 of the sausage and then 1/3 of the cheese. Repeat the layer.
5. Pour the whisked egg mix over.
6. Cook for 5–7 hours or until the top is browned or the eggs are set.

Puerco Pibil

Prep Time: 10 minutes   **Cook Time:** Low for 6-8 hours

Slow Cooker: 4-quarts

Serving Size: 314 g   **Serves:** 10

Calories: 400

Total Fat: 13.9 g **Saturated Fat:** 73.6 g; **Trans Fat:** 0.2 g

Protein: 60.3 g

Total Carbs: 5.9 g; **Dietary Fibre:** 1.8 g; **Sugars:** 3.5 g

Net Carbs: 4.1 g

Cholesterol: 166 mg; **Sodium:** 831 mg; **Potassium:** 1148 mg

Vitamin A: 23%; **Vitamin C:** 2%; **Calcium:** 3%; **Iron:** 18%

Ingredients:
- ☐ 1 can (15 ounces) diced fire-roasted tomato
- ☐ 1 medium onion, sliced
- ☐ 1 orange, juiced
- ☐ 1 teaspoon ground black pepper
- ☐ 1 teaspoon ground cumin
- ☐ 1 teaspoon salt
- ☐ 1/4 cup apple cider vinegar
- ☐ 2 tablespoons paprika powder
- ☐ 2 teaspoons salt
- ☐ 5 pounds pork shoulder roast (or 2 smaller roasts)
- ☐ Pinch nutmeg
- ☐ Water

Directions:
1. In a small mixing bowl, combine the cumin, annatto, nutmeg, and 1 teaspoon of the salt.
2. Stir a little bit of water until the spices become a thick, paste-like consistency.

3. Sauté the onions with 1 tablespoon of fat in a skillet over medium heat until soft. Add the tomatoes and cook for a few minutes until soft.
4. Season the pork with salt.
5. Mix the juice of the orange and the cider vinegar in the slow cooker. Add the cumin paste, stirring until dissolved.
6. Put the pork over the liquid. Top with the onion-tomato mixture.
7. Cover and cook for about 6–8 hours on low, or longer if desired.
8. Skim the excess fat off the top while the dish is still warm. Or refrigerate and the fat will solidify on top and can be easily scooped off.
9. Enjoy with a couple of eggs for breakfast.

Shredded Chicken and Bacon

Prep Time: 10 minutes	**Cook Time:** Low for 8 hours

Slow Cooker: 3-4-quarts

Serving Size: 189 g   **Serves:** 5

Calories: 545

Total Fat: 38.8 g **Saturated Fat:** 8 g; **Trans Fat:** 0 g

Protein: 47.1 g

Total Carbs: 1.9 g; **Dietary Fibre:** 1.1 g; **Sugars:** 0 g

Net Carbs: 3 g

Cholesterol: 144 mg; **Sodium:** 1813 mg; **Potassium:** 456 mg

Vitamin A: 4%; **Vitamin C**: 2%; **Calcium**: 7%; **Iron**: 22%

Ingredients:
- 10 bacon slices
- 5 chicken breasts
- 2 tablespoons dried thyme
- 1 tablespoon dried oregano
- 1 tablespoon dried rosemary
- 1 tablespoon salt
- 8 tablespoons canola oil (5 tablespoons after cooking and 3 tablespoons for the slow cooker)

Directions:
1. Place all of the ingredients in the cooker. Mix together.
2. Cover and cook for about 8 hours on low.
3. When cooked, shred the meat. Mix with 3 tablespoons canola oil.

Spicy Coffee Beef Stew

Prep Time: 15 minutes	**Cook Time:** Low for 6-8 hours
Slow Cooker: 4-quarts	
Serving Size: 238 g	**Serves:** 6-8
Calories: 374	
Total Fat: 12.6 g **Saturated Fat:** 4.6 g; **Trans Fat:** 0 g	
Protein: 58.3 g	
Total Carbs: 4.3 g; **Dietary Fibre:** 1.9 g; **Sugars:** 0.7 g	
Net Carbs: 2.4 g	
Cholesterol: 169 mg; **Sodium:** 361 mg; **Potassium:** 898 mg	
Vitamin A: 23%; **Vitamin C:** 6%; **Calcium:** 3%; **Iron:** 203%	

Ingredients:
- [ ] 1 beef (about 2 1/2 pounds) roast (eye, brisket, or chuck)
- [ ] 1/2 large red onion, thickly sliced
- [ ] 3/4 cup strong brewed coffee, preferably cold brewed
- [ ] 1 tablespoons balsamic vinegar

For the spice paste:
- [ ] 1 teaspoon cumin
- [ ] 1 teaspoon oregano
- [ ] 1/2 teaspoon salt, or to taste
- [ ] 1/8 teaspoon cinnamon
- [ ] 2 teaspoons cocoa powder
- [ ] 3 tablespoons ancho chili powder
- [ ] 4 garlic cloves, minced or pressed

Optional:
- [ ] 1/2 teaspoon chipotle powder, for a spicy dish

Directions:
1. Combine all of the spice paste ingredients in a mixing bowl. Add enough water to form a loose paste consistency. Rub all sides of the beef with the spice paste.
2. Spread the onion in the bottom of the cooker. Place the beef on top of the onions.

3. Stir the coffee and the vinegar together. Pour over the roast.
4. Cover and cook for about 6-8 hours on low or until very tender.

Simpler variation:
Use a pre-made spice mix, such as Penzeys Chili 9000 or VSpicery Cocoa Loco instead of the spice mix.

Sweet and Salty Casserole

Prep Time: 20 minutes   **Cook Time:** Low for 6-8 hours

Slow Cooker: 6-quarts

Serving Size: 168 g   **Serves:** 14

Calories: 401

Total Fat: 33 g **Saturated Fat:** 9.7 g; **Trans Fat:** 0.1 g

Protein: 15.9 g

Total Carbs: 11.8 g; **Dietary Fibre:** 2.1 g; **Sugars:** 3 g

Net Carbs: 9.7 g

Cholesterol: 240 mg; **Sodium:** 620 mg; **Potassium:** 535 mg

Vitamin A: 17%; **Vitamin C:** 47%; **Calcium:** 4%; **Iron:** 11%

Ingredients:

- 6 ounces bacon, chopped
- 1 pound sweet potatoes peeled and shredded
- 1/2-pound sausage crumbled
- 3/4 teaspoon dry mustard
- 16 large eggs, beaten
- 1/4 teaspoon black pepper, cracked
- 1/4 cup coconut milk, full-fat
- 1/2 cup onion (yellow), diced
- 1/2 cup almond milk
- 1 teaspoon sea salt
- 1 red bell pepper, seeded and diced
- 1 orange bell pepper, seeded and diced
- 1/2 cup canola oil

For greasing:

- 1/2 cup canola oil

For garnish:

- Green onions

Directions:

1. Grease the slow cooker with the canola oil.
2. In a skillet, cook the bacon, sausage, and onion for about 10–12 minutes over medium-high heat or until the onion is soft and the sausage is browned.
3. Put the sweet potatoes in the slow cooker. Press down lightly. Add in the cooked meat and onion mix with the grease. Add in the red bell pepper.
4. In a large mixing bowl, whisk the milk, eggs, 1/2 cup canola oil, mustard, salt, and pepper together. Pour the mix into the slow cooker.
5. Cover and cook for 6–8 hours on low.

Ham Hocks and Kale

Prep Time: 20 minutes	**Cook Time:** Low for 6-8 hours

Slow Cooker: 3-4-quarts

Serving Size: 248 g   **Serves:** 8

Calories: 348

Total Fat: 29.4 g **Saturated Fat:** 5.1 g; **Trans Fat:** 0 g

Protein: 12 g

Total Carbs: 11.9 g; **Dietary Fibre:** 1.8 g; **Sugars:** 0.7 g

Net Carbs: 10.1 g

Cholesterol: 27 mg; **Sodium:** 159 mg; **Potassium:** 650 mg

Vitamin A: 310%; **Vitamin C:** 203%; **Calcium:** 14%; **Iron:** 11%

Ingredients:

- [ ] 12 cups kale leaves, tough stems and ribs discarded, torn into 2-inch pieces
- [ ] 1 ham hock (meaty smoked), or 4-5 slices (about 8 ounces) ham hock
- [ ] 1 cup chicken broth, low sodium or homemade
- [ ] 1 1/2 cups water
- [ ] 1 onion, thinly sliced
- [ ] 1/4 teaspoon cayenne pepper, or to taste
- [ ] 2 tablespoons apple cider vinegar, plus more to serve
- [ ] 2 tablespoons bacon grease, canola oil, or vegetable oil
- [ ] Hot sauce, for serving
- [ ] Salt and pepper
- [ ] 1 cup, divided

Directions:

1. Put the ham in a microwave-safe bowl. Cover with the water and the chicken broth. Cover and then microwave for about 3 minutes on high or until the liquid is bubbly.
2. Grease the inside of the cooker with ½ cup canola oil. Add the kale into the bottom of the cooker.

3. Over medium-high heat on the stovetop, heat a large pan. Put the remaining 1/2 cup canola oil. Sauté the onion for about 5–7 minutes or until lightly browned and translucent. Add into the cooker.
4. Add the microwaved ham and the cooking liquid into the cooker. Stir.
5. Cover and cook for about 6-8 hours on low until the kale is tender and nice.
6. After 6–8 hours, remove the ham from the cooker. Shred the meat, discarding the bones and the skin. Return to the cooker. Set the cooker to warm.
7. Serve directly from the pot with a bottle of hot sauce and vinegar.

Slow Roasted Beef Chuck

Prep Time: 20 minutes   **Cook Time:** Low for 8 hours, plus 20 minutes

Slow Cooker: 6-quarts

Serving Size: 343 g   **Serves:** 8

Calories: 1040

Total Fat: 82.4 g **Saturated Fat:** 27.9 g; **Trans Fat:** 0.1 g

Protein: 60.7 g

Total Carbs: 7.5 g; **Dietary Fibre:** 2.8 g; **Sugars:** 2 g

Net Carbs: 4.7 g

Cholesterol: 234 mg; **Sodium:** 173 mg; **Potassium:** 751 mg

Vitamin A: 34%; **Vitamin C:** 32%; **Calcium:** 12%; **Iron:** 66%

Ingredients:
- 4 pounds beef chuck roast
- 4 each garlic cloves
- 2 celery ribs, cut into chunks
- 10 sprigs fresh thyme
- 3/4 cup canola oil
- 1 small onion, cut into chunks
- 1 small head cauliflower, leaves removed and cut into florets
- 1 large carrot, peeled and cut into chunks
- 1 each bay leaf
- 1 cup red wine, good quality
- Salt and pepper, to taste

Directions:
1. Generously season the beef with salt and pepper.
2. Over medium-high heat, heat a large sauté skillet or pan. Add the oil, swirl it around. Quickly pan sear the beef until a nice brown crust forms. Flip the beef over to sear the other side. Continue flipping until all the sides are browned. Put into the cooker.

3. Pour the wine into the still very hot pan. This will boil quickly, releasing the flavor of the morsels in the bottom of the skillet or pan. Swirl the pan around and scraping the morsels with a wooden spoon. Pour the wine over the beef in the cooker.
4. Add the thyme, garlic, and bay leaves, making sure they are submerged in the liquid.
5. Except for the cauliflower, add the remaining of the vegetables, pushing them on the sides of the roast. Season with salt and pepper.
6. Close and cook for about 8 hours on low.
7. After 8 hours, add your cauliflower into the cooker, pushing the florets under the surface of the liquid.
8. Season with a little salt and pepper.
9. Cover and cook for another 20 minutes.

Easy Morning Pie

Prep Time: 10 minutes   **Cook Time:** Low for 8-10 hours

Slow Cooker: 4-quarts

Serving Size: 144 g   **Serves:** 6

Calories: 449

Total Fat: 36.7 g **Saturated Fat:** 10.1 g; **Trans Fat:** 0.2 g

Protein: 22.9 g

Total Carbs: 7.1 g; **Dietary Fibre:** 1.2 g; **Sugars:** 2.8 g

Net Carbs: 5.9 g

Cholesterol: 282 mg; **Sodium:** 656 mg; **Potassium:** 434 mg

Vitamin A: 8%; **Vitamin C:** 5%; **Calcium:** 14%; **Iron:** 16%

Ingredients:

- [ ] 1-pound pork sausage, broken up
- [ ] 8 eggs, whisked
- [ ] 2 teaspoons dried basil
- [ ] 1 yellow onion, diced
- [ ] 1 tablespoon garlic powder
- [ ] 1 sweet potato or yam, shredded
- [ ] 4 tablespoon canola oil

To taste:
- [ ] Salt & Pepper

Optional:
- [ ] Vegetables (squash, peppers, etc.) you want to put in.

Directions:
1. Grease the slow cooker with the canola oil.
2. Put all of the ingredients into the slow cooker and mix well.
3. Cook for 6–8 hour on low or until the pork sausage is cooked through.

4. Slice into 6–8 pies.

Lunch

These recipes are designed to be quick and easy to make. They are flexible enough to be used as an enjoyable lunch time meal or a delectable dinner.

Herbed Salmon

Prep Time: 15 minutes	**Cook Time:** Low for 2 1/2 hours; high for 1 1/2 hours

Slow Cooker: 3-quarts
Serving Size: 148 g   **Serves:** 4
Calories: 306
Total Fat: 24.5 g **Saturated Fat:** 3.5 g; **Trans Fat:** 0 g
Protein: 6 g
Total Carbs: 1.5 g; **Dietary Fibre:** 0 g; **Sugars:** 0 g
Net Carbs: 1.5 g
Cholesterol: 50 mg; **Sodium:** 99 mg; **Potassium:** 469 mg
Vitamin A: 6%; **Vitamin C:** 7%; **Calcium:** 5%; **Iron:** 5%

Ingredients:

- ☐ 1 pound (4 fillets) salmon fillet
- ☐ 1 tablespoon canola oil
- ☐ 1/4 teaspoon kosher salt (or any salt)
- ☐ 2 garlic cloves, pressed or finely chopped
- ☐ 2-3 tablespoon lime juice
- ☐ 3/4 cup cilantro, stems removed and chopped

For greasing the slow cooker:

- ☐ 4 tablespoons canola oil

Directions:

1. Grease the slow cooker with the canola oil.
2. With the skin side down, place the salmon fillets into the slow cooker, making sure not to overlap the fillets.

3. In a small bowl, combine the lime juice, garlic, cilantro, canola oil, and salt. Pour over the salmon.
4. Cook for 2 1/2 hours on low or 1–1 1/2 hours on high.

Scallops Florentine

Prep Time: 10 minutes **Cook Time:** Low for 1-1 3/4 hours	
Slow Cooker: 3 1/2 or 4-quart	
Serving Size: 360 g **Serves:** 2	
Calories: 327	
Total Fat: 13.5 g **Saturated Fat:** 7.7 g; **Trans Fat:** 0 g	
Protein: 42.2 g	
Total Carbs: 11.1 g; **Dietary Fibre:** 3.1 g; **Sugars:** 0.6 g	
Net Carbs: 8 g	
Cholesterol: 97 mg; **Sodium:** 730 mg; **Potassium:** 1356 mg	
Vitamin A: 276%; **Vitamin C:** 76%; **Calcium:** 45%; **Iron:** 25%	

Ingredients:

- ☐ 12 ounces (340 g) sea scallops
- ☐ 10 ounces (280 g) spinach, frozen, thawed, chopped, squeezed dry
- ☐ 1/4 cup (60 ml) heavy cream
- ☐ 1/4 cup (25 g) Parmesan cheese, grated
- ☐ 1 tablespoon (7 g) Old Bay seafood seasoning
- ☐ 1 garlic clove, crushed

Directions:

1. Put the spinach into the slow cooker.
2. Add in the cream, cheese, garlic, and the seasoning. Stir the mixture well to combine. Cover the slow cooker with the lid. Cook for about 30–45 minutes on low or until the spinach is warm.
3. In a single layer, put in the scallops over the warmed spinach. Re-cover. Continue cooking for about 1 hour.

Lemon Mustard Salmon Steaks

Prep Time: 10 minutes   **Cook Time:** Low for 1 3/4 hours

Slow Cooker: 3-quarts

Serving Size: 325 g   **Serves:** 2

Calories: 624

Total Fat: 49.4 g **Saturated Fat:** 24.2 g; **Trans Fat:** 0 g

Protein: 45.3 g

Total Carbs: 1.8 g; **Dietary Fibre:** 0.7 g; **Sugars:** 1 g

Net Carbs: 1.1 g

Cholesterol: 192 mg; **Sodium:** 885 mg; **Potassium:** 967 mg

Vitamin A: 32%; **Vitamin C:** 38%; **Calcium:** 11%; **Iron:** 11%

Ingredients:

- 2 salmon steaks (about 455 g or 1 pound)
- 2 tablespoons (8 g) fresh parsley, chopped
- 6 tablespoons butter
- 5 teaspoon Dijon mustard
- 5 tablespoon lemon juice
- 5 pinch salt

Directions:

1. Combine the mustard, butter, lemon juice, and salt in the slow cooker. Cover and cook for about 30-45 minutes on low. Stir together after.

2. Put the salmon steaks into the slow cooker with the sauce. Turn the fish once or twice to coat. Re-cover. Continue cooking for 1 hour on low. When cooked, transfer the salmon steaks in serving plates. Spoon the sauce over the salmon. Sprinkle with the parsley.

Chicken Bacon Sandwiches

Prep Time: 10 minutes	**Cook Time:** High for 4 hours, Low for 6-8 hours

Slow Cooker: 4-quarts
Serving Size: 312 g   **Serves:** 6
Calories: 820
Total Fat: 67 g **Saturated Fat:** 30 g; **Trans Fat:** 0 g
Protein: 50 g
Total Carbs: 5 g; **Dietary Fibre:** 0 g; **Sugars:** 3 g
Net Carbs: 5 g
Cholesterol: 245 mg; **Sodium:** 1090 mg; **Potassium:** 810 mg
Vitamin A: 30%; **Vitamin C:** 4%; **Calcium:** 30%; **Iron:** 2%

Ingredients:
- ☐ 1 1/2 cups Colby Jack cheese, shredded
- ☐ 10 ounces bacon, cooked, broken into pieces
- ☐ 2 ounces dry ranch dressing mix (2 packets)
- ☐ 2 pounds chicken breasts, boneless skinless
- ☐ 8 ounces cream cheese
- ☐ 8 ounces Philadelphia cream cheese with bacon
- ☐ Nonstick cooking spray

For serving:
- ☐ 6 low carb buns or rolls

Directions:
1. Grease the slow cooker with the cooking spray; place the chicken.
2. In a medium bowl, combine the bacon, ranch dressing, bacon cream cheese, and cream cheese; spread in the slow cooker.
3. Cook for 4 hours on high or 6-8 hours on low, watching closely so it doesn't overcook.
4. Using 2 forks, shred the chicken, stir well until coated with the sauce.
5. Serve the chicken between low carb rolls or buns topped with the shredded cheese. If desired, broil for about 45 seconds, watching closely, until the cheese is melted.

Peanut Saucy Chicken Wings

Prep Time: 25 minutes	**Cook Time:** Low for 5-6 hours; high for 2 1/2-3 hours

Slow Cooker: 3 1/2 or 4-quart

Serving Size: 115 g   **Serves:** 12

Calories: 217

Total Fat: 10.4 g **Saturated Fat**: 2.6 g; **Trans Fat**: 0 g

Protein: 27.2 g

Total Carbs: 4.1 g; **Dietary Fibre**: 1.2 g; **Sugars**: 0 g

Net Carbs: 2.9 g

Cholesterol: 76 mg; **Sodium**: 451 mg; **Potassium**: 309 mg

Vitamin A: 2%; **Vitamin C**: 1%; **Calcium**: 2%; **Iron**: 11%

Ingredients:
- ☐ 24 pieces (about 2 1/4 pounds) chicken wings

For the chicken coating:
- ☐ 1/2 cup salsa, bottled
- ☐ 2 tablespoons peanut butter, creamy
- ☐ 2 teaspoons soy sauce
- ☐ 1 tablespoon lime juice
- ☐ 2 teaspoons ginger, freshly grated

For the peanut sauce:
- ☐ 1/4 cup sugar substitute (such as Splenda), granular, heat-stable, no-calorie.
- ☐ 1/4 cup peanut butter, creamy
- ☐ 3 tablespoons soy sauce
- ☐ 2 garlic cloves, minced
- ☐ 3 tablespoons water

Directions:

1. Put the chicken in the slow cooker.
2. In a small mixing bowl, combine all the chicken coating ingredients. Pour over the chicken and toss wings to coat. Cover the slow cooker.
3. Cook for 5–6 hours on low or 2 ½–3 hours on high.
4. Meanwhile, in a small-size saucepan, whisk all of the peanut sauce ingredients. Heat over medium-low until the sauce is smooth, occasionally whisking. Remove from heat and set aside. The sauce will thicken as it cools down.
5. Drain the cooked chicken wings. Discard the cooking juice. Return the chicken to the slow cooker. Pour in the peanut sauce. Stir gently. Keep warm for not more than 2 hours on low.

Caesar Sandwiches

Prep Time: 10 minutes	**Cook Time:** Low for 4-6 hours, plus high for 30 minutes

Slow Cooker: 3-4-quarts

Serving Size: 317 g   **Serves:** 4

Calories:840

Total Fat: 71 g **Saturated Fat:** 16 g; **Trans Fat:** 0 g

Protein: 44 g

Total Carbs: 3 g; **Dietary Fibre:** 1 g; **Sugars:** 2 g

Net Carbs: 2 g

Cholesterol: 220 mg; **Sodium:** 980 mg; **Potassium:** 540 mg

Vitamin A: 60%; **Vitamin C:** 25%; **Calcium:** 20%; **Iron:** 20%

Ingredients:
- ☐ 2 pounds chicken thighs, boneless, skinless
- ☐ 1/2-1 cup of your preferred Caesar dressing
- ☐ 1/2 cup Parmesan cheese, shredded, plus more for topping
- ☐ 1/4 cup fresh parsley, chopped (or 2 teaspoons dried parsley)
- ☐ 1/2 teaspoon ground pepper
- ☐ 2 cups shredded romaine lettuce

For serving:
- ☐ 4 low carb hamburger buns

Directions:
1. Place the chicken in the slow cooker; add 1 to 2 cups water, cover and cook for 4–6 hours on low.
2. With a slotted spoon, remove the chicken and drain the water from the slow cooker. Place the chicken on a cutting board and pull into shreds.

3. Return the chicken to the cooker; add the dressing, cheese, parsley, and the pepper. Stir until well-mixed. Cover and cook for 30 minutes on high or until hot.
4. Spoon about 1/4 cup into the buns, top with parmesan cheese, then lettuce; serve.

Peppery Sausage Stew

Prep Time: 20 minutes   **Cook Time:** Low for 6 hours

Slow Cooker: 4-quarts

Serving Size: 181 g   **Serves:** 6

Calories: 230

Total Fat: 18 g **Saturated Fat:** 6 g; **Trans Fat:** 0 g

Protein: 9 g

Total Carbs: 8 g; **Dietary Fibre:** 2 g; **Sugars:** 3 g

Net Carbs: 6 g

Cholesterol: 45 mg; **Sodium:** 450 mg; **Potassium:** 430 mg

Vitamin A: 20%; **Vitamin C:** 110%; **Calcium:** 4%; **Iron:** 6%

Ingredients:
- 1 can (14 ounces) diced tomatoes
- 1 green pepper, chopped
- 1 medium onion, chopped
- 1 pound Italian sausage, mild chicken, cooked, chopped
- 1 red pepper, chopped
- 1 tablespoon dried oregano
- 1 yellow pepper, chopped
- 1/4 cup fresh basil, chopped
- 2 tablespoons tomato paste
- 6 cloves garlic, minced

Directions:
1. Add sausage, onion, garlic, peppers, oregano and basil to the slow cooker.
2. Mix the tomatoes and the tomato paste; add to the slow cooker.
3. Cook for 6 hours on low.
4. About 3 hours, cut the sausages into bite-sized pieces; stir to mix.
5. Serve over cauliflower rice.

Chicken-Chorizo Slow Soup

Prep Time: 10 minutes	**Cook Time:** High for 3 hours, plus 30 mins

Slow Cooker: 6-quarts

Serving Size: 464 g   **Serves:** 8

Calories: 801

Total Fat: 62.5 g **Saturated Fat:** 17.7 g; **Trans Fat:** 0 g

Protein: 53 g

Total Carbs: 7.3 g; **Dietary Fibre:** 1.2 g; **Sugars:** 3.8 g

Net Carbs: 6.1 g

Cholesterol: 172mg; **Sodium:** 1380 mg; **Potassium:** 750 mg

Vitamin A: 22%; **Vitamin C:** 28%; **Calcium:** 5%; **Iron:** 14%

Ingredients:
- ☐ 2 pounds chicken thighs, boneless, skinless
- ☐ 1 pound chorizo
- ☐ 4 cups chicken stock
- ☐ 2 tablespoons Worcestershire sauce
- ☐ 2 tablespoons garlic, minced
- ☐ 2 tablespoons red hot sauce
- ☐ 1 cup heavy cream
- ☐ 1 can stewed tomatoes
- ☐ 1 cup canola oil, plus 2 tbsp.

For garnish:
- ☐ Parmesan cheese, shaved
- ☐ Sour cream

Directions:
1. In a skillet, cook the chorizo until browned in the 1 cup canola oil.
2. Grease the slow cooker with the 2 tablespoons of canola oil.
3. Layer the ingredients into the slow cooker according to the order – chicken, chorizo with the grease, and then the remaining ingredients.

4. Cook for about 3 hours on high.
5. Remove the thighs from the slow cooker. Pull apart with forks. Return to the slow cooker.
6. Cook for about 30 minutes more. When cooked, serve with parmesan cheese and sour cream.

Chicken Buffalo Sliders

Prep Time: 10 minutes   **Cook Time:** Low for 8 hours, High for 4 hours, plus 30 minutes

Slow Cooker: 4-quarts

Serving Size: 353 g   **Serves:** 4

Calories: 450

Total Fat: 36 g **Saturated Fat:** 7 g; **Trans Fat:** 0 g

Protein: 22 g

Total Carbs: 10 g; **Dietary Fibre:** <1 g; **Sugars:** 3 g

Net Carbs: <9 g

Cholesterol: 85 mg; **Sodium:** 3670 mg; **Potassium:** 660 mg

Vitamin A: 10%; **Vitamin C:** 10%; **Calcium:** 180%; **Iron:** 4%

Ingredients:
- ☐ 1 cup blue cheese dressing, or to taste
- ☐ 1 cup water
- ☐ 2 cups cabbage, coleslaw or thinly sliced
- ☐ 2 cups hot sauce, Franks buffalo, divided
- ☐ 2-3 boneless skinless chicken breasts
- ☐ 6-8 low carb dinner rolls or slider buns
- ☐ Blue cheese, crumbled crumbles, optional

Directions:
1. Place the chicken, 1 cup of the hot sauce, and water in the cooker; cover and cook for 8 hour on low or 4 hours on high. When cooked, drain the cooker, and shred the chicken using 2 forks.
2. Add the remaining hot sauce, stir to combine, cover and cook for 30 minutes more.
3. Serve on the rolls or buns, top with the slaw, with the blue cheese if using, and the dressing. Serve warm or at room temperature.

Beef Roast on Fritters

Prep Time: 16 minutes	**Cook Time:** Low for 8-10 hours

Slow Cooker: 4-quarts

Serving Size: 74 g   **Serves:** 16

Calories: 300

Total Fat: 24 g **Saturated Fat:** 5 g; **Trans Fat:** 0 g

Protein: 11 g

Total Carbs: 9 g; **Dietary Fibre:** 1 g; **Sugars:** 2 g

Net Carbs: 8 g

Cholesterol: 60 mg; **Sodium:** 220 mg; **Potassium:** 260 mg

Vitamin A: 6%; **Vitamin C:** 10%; **Calcium:** 6%; **Iron:** 8%

Ingredients:
For the beef roast:
- ☐ 1 1/2 ounces beef chuck roast
- ☐ 1 can (15 ounces) diced tomatoes
- ☐ 1 jalapeño, minced
- ☐ 1 onion, sliced
- ☐ 1 tablespoon canola oil
- ☐ 1 teaspoon ancho chili powder
- ☐ 1/2 teaspoon cumin
- ☐ 3 garlic cloves, minced
- ☐ Salt and pepper

For the fritters:
- ☐ 1 1/2 teaspoon sugar (3/4 packet stevia)
- ☐ 1 cup cornmeal
- ☐ 1 cup vegetable oil
- ☐ 1 jalapeno, minced
- ☐ 1/2 cup cheddar cheese, finely shredded
- ☐ 1/4 cup 2% milk
- ☐ 2 eggs
- ☐ 3/4 teaspoon salt

Directions:

1. Over medium high heat, heat the skillet. Season both sides of the roast with the salt and the pepper. Add the canola oil; sear the beef for about 1-2 minutes per side.
2. Place the seared beef in the cooker; season with the cumin, ancho chili powder, a little more salt and pepper. Top with the remaining ingredients. Cook on low for about 8-10 hours on low or until easily shredded with a fork.
3. Just before serving cook the fritters. Heat the oil until 375F.
4. In a mixing bowl, stir the milk, cornmeal, sugar substitute, eggs, and salt until well combined. Add the cheese and the jalapeno; stir to incorporate.
5. Take a spoonful of the mixture; flatten between your hands. Very carefully slide into the hot oil; fry for 2 minutes per side. Drain in paper towel lined plate.
6. Serve the shredded beef over the fritter. Enjoy while they're warm.

Tortilla-less Chicken Slow Soup

Prep Time: 20 minutes	**Cook Time:** Low for 8 hours, high for 4 hours

Slow Cooker: 4-quarts
Serving Size: 257 g **Serves:** 12
Calories: 340
Total Fat: 24.4 g **Saturated Fat:** 3.2 g; **Trans Fat:** 0 g
Protein: 22 g
Total Carbs: 11.6 g; **Dietary Fibre:** 4.1 g; **Sugars:** 6.7 g
Net Carbs: 7.5 g
Cholesterol: 49 mg; **Sodium:** 338 mg; **Potassium:** 599 mg
Vitamin A: 11%; **Vitamin C:** 44%; **Calcium:** 3%; **Iron:** 11%

Ingredients:

- ☐ 4 boneless, skinless chicken breast
- ☐ 1 can (28 ounces) diced tomatoes
- ☐ 1 can (4 ounces) diced green chilies
- ☐ 1 jalapeño, diced
- ☐ 1 red bell pepper, diced
- ☐ 1 teaspoon ground cumin
- ☐ 1 yellow onion, diced
- ☐ 1 cup canola oil, plus ¼ cup
- ☐ 2 teaspoons chili powder
- ☐ 3 cloves garlic, minced
- ☐ 4 cups chicken broth
- ☐ Black pepper to taste

For garnish:

- ☐ Chopped cilantro
- ☐ Guacamole

Directions:

1. In a large skillet over medium heat, preheat the ¼ cup canola oil.
2. Put the onion, jalapeno, bell pepper, and onions into the skillet. Sauté until the onions are translucent.

3. Pour the onion mixture into the cooker. Put the remaining ingredients into the cooker.
4. Close the cover and cook.
5. When cooked, remove the chicken with tongs and put in a cutting board or plate.
6. Using a knife or 2 forks, shred the chicken into bite-sized pieces.
7. Return the shredded chicken into the cooker. Stir to mix.
8. Spoon the soup into serving bowls. Top with guacamole and cilantro and serve.

Veggie Noodles Asian Chicken

Prep Time: 30 minutes	**Cook Time:** Low for 3 1/2-4 hours

Slow Cooker: 4-quarts

Serving Size: 472 g   **Serves**: 6

Calories: 1020

Total Fat: 83.7 g **Saturated Fat**: 19.9 g; **Trans Fat**: 0 g

Protein: 64.1 g

Total Carbs: 11.9 g; **Dietary Fibre**: 3.7g; **Sugars**: 5.4 g

Net Carbs: 8.2 g

Cholesterol: 156 mg; **Sodium**: 821 mg; **Potassium**: 1001 mg

Vitamin A: 61%; **Vitamin C**: 33%; **Calcium**: 7%; **Iron**: 27%

Ingredients:
- ☐ 2 pounds chicken breast or thigh, skinned
- ☐ 2 teaspoons fish sauce
- ☐ 2 medium zucchini, spiralized
- ☐ 2 heaping tablespoons peanut butter or sunflower butter
- ☐ 2 cloves garlic, smashed, minced, or 1 teaspoon garlic powder
- ☐ 1 teaspoon red pepper flakes
- ☐ 1 teaspoon cayenne pepper
- ☐ 1 tablespoon ginger, freshly minced or 2 teaspoons ginger powder
- ☐ 1 tablespoon coconut aminos or wheat-free tamari
- ☐ 1 large carrot, shredded
- ☐ 1 cup coconut milk
- ☐ 1 cup chicken stock
- ☐ 1 small bunch green onions (for sauce and garnish)
- ☐ Salt and pepper, to season
- ☐ 1 cup canola oil, plus ½ cup

Optional:
- ☐ 1 handful bean sprouts, washed
- ☐ Chopped cilantro, for garnish

☐ Chopped cashews, for garnish

Directions:

1. Season the chicken with salt and pepper. If desired, season with a little cayenne pepper and ginger powder. If you have time, brown the chicken in a cast iron skillet with the 1/2 cup canola oil to develop the flavors.
2. Pour the chicken stock, 1 cup canola oil, and the coconut milk in the cooker. Stir well until well combined.
3. Add the coconut aminos, fish sauce, peanut butter, garlic, ginger, 2 green onions (greens and whites), red pepper, and cayenne. Stir well until the peanut butter is dissolved completely.
4. Place the chicken in the base liquid in the cooker.
5. Turn the zucchinis into noodles with a spiral slicer. Shred the carrots. Wash the bean sprouts, if using. In a large container, toss them well together.
6. Balance or nest the vegetables on top of the meat and liquid base in the cooker, and very lightly press down. The goal is to steam the veggies, not to stew them.
7. Cover the lid and cook.
8. To serve, remove the vegetables first, straining any liquid, and setting them aside.
9. Remove the chicken. Cut into strips. Debone if needed. Return the chicken strips into the cooker. Mix well.
10. Pour the meat and sauce over the vegetables.
11. Garnish with green onions, and if desired, cashews and cilantro.

Kielbasa with Cabbage

Prep Time: 5 minutes   **Cook Time:** Low for 8 hours

Slow Cooker: 4-quarts

Serving Size: 513 g   **Serves:** 6

Calories: 274

Total Fat: 30.5 g **Saturated Fat:** 7.2 g; **Trans Fat:** 0 g

Protein: 12.4 g

Total Carbs: 11.8 g; **Dietary Fibre:** 3.4 g; **Sugars:** 4.7 g

Net Carbs: 8.4 g

Cholesterol: 53mg; **Sodium:** 1279 mg; **Potassium:** 266 mg

Vitamin A: 2%; **Vitamin C:** 93%; **Calcium:** 5%; **Iron:** 9%

Ingredients:

- ☐ 1 cabbage head small, (about 2 1/2 pounds), cored, cut into wedges
- ☐ 1 cup chicken broth
- ☐ 1 medium onion, halved, thinly sliced
- ☐ 1 pound kielbasa, cut into 3-inch pieces
- ☐ 1 tablespoon brown mustard
- ☐ 1/2 cup canola oil
- ☐ 1/2 teaspoon black pepper
- ☐ 1/2 teaspoon kosher salt

Directions:

1. Coat the slow cooker with the canola oil.
2. Except for the kielbasa, add the rest of the ingredients to the cooker; toss until the cabbage is well coated. Top the the cabbage mixture with the kielbasa.
3. Cook for 7 hours on low; stir then cook for another 1 hour.

Greek Chicken

Prep Time: 30-45 minutes   **Cook Time:** Low for 6-8 hours, high for 4 hours

Slow Cooker: 3-4-quarts

Serving Size: 433 g   **Serves:** 4

Calories: 800

Total Fat: 64.4 g **Saturated Fat:** 12.2 g; **Trans Fat:** 0 g

Protein: 46.1 g

Total Carbs: 7.7 g; **Dietary Fibre:** 1.9 g; **Sugars:** 3 g

Net Carbs: 5.8 g

Cholesterol: 141 mg; **Sodium:** 634 mg; **Potassium:** 708 mg

Vitamin A: 92%; **Vitamin C:** 60%; **Calcium:** 15%; **Iron:** 19%

Ingredients:

- 4 chicken breasts, boneless
- 6 ounces fresh spinach
- 1 1/2 teaspoon fresh oregano (or 1/2 teaspoon dried oregano)
- 1 cup chicken stock
- 1 tablespoon canola oil (or your preferred fat)
- 1/2 cup white wine
- 1/2 onion, diced
- 1/2 red pepper, cut into thin strips
- 1/3 cup feta cheese (leave out if you are allergic to dairy)
- 2 pepperoncini peppers, cut into thin strips
- 2 teaspoons minced garlic
- Salt and pepper, to taste
- Squeeze of lemon

Optional toppings:

- Fresh oregano or mint

- ☐ Fresh parsley
- ☐ Squeeze of fresh lemon

Directions:

1. In the middle of one side of each breast, cut a deep slit, creating a deep pocket in the meat. Generously season each side of the breasts with salt and pepper. Set aside.
2. Pour ½ cup of the canola oil in a skillet over medium heat. Sauté the onions and the peppers for about 1-2 minutes or until they are no longer raw. Add the garlic and the spinach. Cook until the spinach is just wilted. Add the oregano and a pinch of salt and pepper. Remove from heat.
3. If using feta cheese, stuff a heaping 1 teaspoon in the pockets in the chicken. Make sure to stuff it as far back as you can.
4. Divide the spinach mixture into the number of your breasts and stuff them into the breasts.
5. Put the stuffed chicken into the cooker. Squeeze a small amount of lemon juice over the chicken.
6. Add the wine, canola oil, and the chicken stock.
7. Cover and cook for about 6–8 hours on low or for about 4 hours on high.
8. When cooked, top with the optional toppings and serve.

Herbed-Port Slow Roast

Prep Time: 15 minutes   **Cook Time:** Low for 8-10 hours; high for 4-5 hours

Slow Cooker: 3 1/2 or 4-quart

Serving Size: 182g   **Serves:** 10

Calories: 280

Total Fat: 8.6 g **Saturated Fat:** 3.2 g; **Trans Fat:** 0 g

Protein: 41.7 g

Total Carbs: 6.4 g; **Dietary Fibre:** 0.6 g; **Sugars:** 3 g

Net Carbs: 5.8 g

Cholesterol: 122 mg; **Sodium:** 226mg; **Potassium:** 652 mg

Vitamin A: 2%; **Vitamin C:** 12%; **Calcium:** 1%; **Iron:** 145%

Ingredients:

- ☐ 1 piece (2 1/2-3 pounds) beef chuck pot roast
- ☐ 1 can (8-ounce) tomato sauce
- ☐ 1 tablespoon Worcestershire sauce
- ☐ 1 teaspoon dried oregano, crushed
- ☐ 1 teaspoon dried thyme, crushed
- ☐ 1/2 cup (1 medium) onion, chopped
- ☐ 1/2 cup apple juice or port wine
- ☐ 2 garlic cloves; mince
- ☐ 3 tablespoons tapioca, quick-cooking

Optional:

- ☐ Spaghetti squash or zucchini pasta, hot cooked

Directions:

1. Trim the fat from the meat and then place in the slow cooker. If the meat does not fit, cut to fit.
2. In a large mixing bowl, combine the rest of the ingredients. Pour over the meat. Cover slow cooker.
3. Cook for 8-10 hours on low or 4-5 hours on high. When cooked, transfer meat into a serving platter.

4. Skim fat from the gravy. Serve gravy with the pot roast. If desired, serve with hot cooked spaghetti squash or zucchini pasta.

Creamy Chive Chicken

Prep Time: 15 minutes **Cook Time:** Low for 4-5 hours	
Slow Cooker: 3 1/2 or 4-quart	
Serving Size: 168 g **Serves:** 6	
Calories: 379	
Total Fat: 23 g **Saturated Fat:** 11.4 g; **Trans Fat:** 0 g	
Protein: 34.5 g	
Total Carbs: 3.4 g; **Dietary Fibre:** 0 g; **Sugars:** 0 g	
Net Carbs: 3.4 g	
Cholesterol: 142 mg; **Sodium:** 411 mg; **Potassium:** 335 mg	
Vitamin A: 11%; **Vitamin C:** 0%; **Calcium:** 4%; **Iron:** 10%	

Ingredients:

- ☐ 6 (about 1 1/2 pounds) chicken breast halves, skinless, boneless
- ☐ 1 can (1 0 3/4-ounce) condensed golden mushroom soup
- ☐ 1 package (0.7-ounce) Italian salad dressing mix
- ☐ 1/2 cup dry white wine
- ☐ 1/2 of an 8-ounce tub cream cheese with chives and onion
- ☐ 1/4 cup butter

Optional:

- ☐ Spaghetti squash or zucchini pasta, hot cooked
- ☐ Fresh chives, snipped

Directions:

1. Put the chicken into the slow cooker.
2. In a medium saucepan, melt the butter. Add in the dry Italian salad dressing mix. Stir. Pour in the mushroom soup, the wine, and the cream cheese. Stir until well combined. Pour over the chicken in the slow cooker. Cover slow cooker.

3. Cook for 4-5 hours in low. When cooked, serve chicken with the sauce. Sprinkle with chives and with hot cooked spaghetti squash or zucchini pasta, if desired.

Pork Carnitas

Prep Time: 30-45 minutes   **Cook Time:** Low for 5 hours

Slow Cooker: 4-6 quarts

Serving Size: 422 g   **Serves:** 6

Calories: 1061

Total Fat: 85.8 g **Saturated Fat:** 12.7 g; **Trans Fat:** 0 g

Protein: 65.8 g

Total Carbs: 5 g; **Dietary Fibre:** 0.6 g; **Sugars:** 2.7 g

Net Carbs: 4.4 g

Cholesterol: 184 mg; **Sodium:** 841 mg; **Potassium:** 1094 mg

Vitamin A: 5%; **Vitamin C:** 35%; **Calcium:** 6%; **Iron:** 18%

Ingredients:
- [ ] 3 pounds pork loin roast
- [ ] 1 lime
- [ ] 1 tablespoon Adobo seasoning
- [ ] 2 cups chicken stock, organic or homemade
- [ ] 2 oranges
- [ ] 2 tablespoons tomato paste
- [ ] 3-4 crushed garlic cloves
- [ ] 1 canola oil, plus 3/4 cup

For the spice blend:
- [ ] 1 teaspoon garlic powder
- [ ] 1 teaspoon chili powder
- [ ] 1 teaspoon ground cumin
- [ ] 1 teaspoon kosher salt

Directions:
1. Slice the roast into 2-inch steaks, cutting across the grain and leaving all of the fat in place.
2. In a large bowl (large enough to toss the pork steaks), mix the spice blend ingredients. When the spices are blended, add a

couple pieces of the pork steaks and evenly coat. Allow to rest while you heat the skillet.

3. Over medium high-heat, heat a skillet or a thick, large bottomed pan. Add your fat of choice in the skillet. Sear the steak in batches, about 2-3 pieces, depending on the size of your pan. Sear both sides of the steaks.
4. Put the seared steaks into the cooker, while cooking the rest.
5. When all the steaks are seared, pour the stock, adobo seasoning, tomato paste, and garlic cloves in the pan. This will deglaze the pan. Allow to simmer for a couple of minutes, scraping the bits from the bottom of the pan.
6. While the broth is simmering, juice the oranges and the lime. Set aside.
7. Pour the broth over the seared pork in the cooker. Add the orange and lemon juice.
8. Cover and cook for about 5 hours on low.

To make the carnitas:
Shred the meat with forks or a pastry cutter. Caramelize by putting the meat in a skillet with some oil and brown or broil the meat for a few minutes.

Notes:
If your cooker turns off after the timer dings, this will keep the dish warm for a while. However, if the cooker turns to keep warm, this may dry out the meat.

Storing:
If you are not serving the whole meat in one setting, then just cut your needed portion and store the remaining. Also, do not throw away the cooking liquid. You will need it to rehydrate the meat.

Korean Chicken Kimchi

Prep Time: 15 minutes   **Cook Time:** Low for 4-6 hours

Slow Cooker: 2-3 quarts

Serving Size: 294 g   **Serves:** 6

Calories: 348

Total Fat: 13.5 g **Saturated Fat:** 0 g; **Trans Fat:** 0 g

Protein: 44.8 g

Total Carbs: 6.6 g; **Dietary Fibre:** 0 g; **Sugars:** 1.7 g

Net Carbs: 6.6 g

Cholesterol: 135 mg; **Sodium:** 817 mg; **Potassium:** 417 mg

Vitamin A: 4%; **Vitamin C:** 5%; **Calcium:** 4%; **Iron:** 12%

Ingredients:
- [ ] About 2 cups cabbage kimchi, drained
- [ ] 2 pounds chicken thighs, boneless, skinless
- [ ] 6 garlic cloves, pressed or minced
- [ ] 4 scallions, white and green parts separated, sliced
- [ ] 2 teaspoons palm sugar or sweetener of choice (can omit, if necessary)
- [ ] 1 teaspoon grated or minced fresh ginger or 1/4 teaspoon ground ginger, high-quality
- [ ] 1 tablespoons dark sesame oil
- [ ] 1 tablespoon soy sauce (coconut aminos or tamari)
- [ ] 1 cup chicken broth, low-sodium

Directions:
1. Except for the kimchi, chicken, and scallion greens, combine the rest of the ingredients in the cooker.
2. Nestle the chicken on the mixture in the cooker. Spoon some sauce over the top of the chicken.
3. Cover and cook for about 4-6 hours on low. It's preferable to cook this dish closer to 4 hours.
4. Serve over cauliflower rice.

Keto Chili

Prep Time: 30 minutes	**Cook Time:** Low for 6 hours

Slow Cooker: 3 quarts

Serving Size: 292 g   **Serves:** 8

Calories: 320

Total Fat: 12.3 g **Saturated Fat:** 4 g; **Trans Fat:** 0 g

Protein: 39.1 g

Total Carbs: 12.7 g; **Dietary Fibre:** 3.1 g; **Sugars:** 6.7 g

Net Carbs: 9.6 g

Cholesterol: 104 mg; **Sodium:** 588mg; **Potassium:** 1070 mg

Vitamin A: 20%; **Vitamin C:** 77%; **Calcium:** 4%; **Iron:** 14%

Ingredients:
- ☐ 8 pieces bacon, thick-cut
- ☐ 6 ounces tomato paste
- ☐ 300 grams' yellow onion or 1-piece medium onion, chopped
- ☐ 300 grams' green pepper or 3 pieces' small peppers, chopped
- ☐ 2 pounds ground pork
- ☐ 1 pack chili seasoning
- ☐ 1 can diced tomatoes, drained

To taste:
- ☐ Salt
- ☐ Garlic powder
- ☐ Pepper
- ☐ Onion powder
- ☐ Cayenne pepper

Directions:
1. Place the peppers and the onions in the slow cooker.

2. In a skillet, brown the pork. Season with salt and pepper. Drain excess grease. Allow to cool and put in the slow cooker.
3. Cut the bacon into small pieces. Cook, drain excess grease, and put into the slow cooker.
4. Add the tomatoes, tomato paste, and the chili seasoning.
5. Cook for 6 hours on low. When cooked, add seasoning according to taste.

Slow Roast with Dill

Prep Time: 20 minutes	**Cook Time:** Low for 10- 12 hours; high for 5-6 hours, plus 10 minutes

Slow Cooker: 3 1/2 or 4-quart

Serving Size: 273 g   **Serves:** 6

Calories: 468449

Total Fat: 16.7 g **Saturated Fat:** 5.9 g; **Trans Fat:** 0 g

Protein: 70.4 g

Total Carbs: 3.9 g; **Dietary Fibre:** 0 g; **Sugars:** 1.4 g

Net Carbs: 3.9 g

Cholesterol: 204 mg; **Sodium:** 326 mg; **Potassium:** 989 mg

Vitamin A: 1%; **Vitamin C:** 1%; **Calcium:** 5%; **Iron:** 240%

Ingredients:

- ☐ 1 piece (2 1/2-3 pounds) beef chuck pot roast, boneless
- ☐ 2 tablespoons all-purpose flour
- ☐ 1/2 teaspoon coarse salt or 1/4 teaspoon regular salt
- ☐ 1/2 teaspoon black pepper
- ☐ 1/2 cup water
- ☐ 1/2 cup plain yogurt
- ☐ 1 teaspoon dried dill, divided into 3/4 and 1/4 teaspoons
- ☐ 1 tablespoon fresh dill, snipped
- ☐ 1 tablespoon cooking oil

Optional:

- ☐ Spaghetti squash or zucchini pasta, hot cooked

Directions:

1. Trim the fat from the meat. If the meat does not fit in the slow cooker, cut to fit. In a large skillet, brown all the sides of the meat in hot oil. When all the sides are browned, transfer the meat into the slow cooker.

2. Pour in the water, sprinkle the 3/4 teaspoons dried dill, the 1 tablespoon fresh dill, salt, and black pepper. Cover the slow cooker.

3. Cook for 10-12 hours on low or 5-6 hours on high. When cooked, transfer meat into a serving platter and cover with foil to keep warm. Skim the fat off the cooking liquid and measure 1 cup.

4. In a small saucepan, stir the yogurt and the flour together. Stir in the 1 cup cooking juice and the remaining 1/4 teaspoon dried dill. Cook, stirring, until the sauce is bubbly and thick. Pour the sauce over the meat. Serve with cooked spaghetti squash or zucchini pasta, if desired.

Beef Bourgeon

Prep Time: 30 minutes   **Cook Time:** Low for 8 hours, high for 6 hours

Slow Cooker: 3-4-quarts

Serving Size: 369 g   **Serves:** 6

Calories: 656

Total Fat: 52.5 g **Saturated Fat:** 5.8 g; **Trans Fat:** 0 g

Protein: 32.8 g

Total Carbs: 14 g; **Dietary Fibre:** 3.5 g; **Sugars:** 5.3 g

Net Carbs: 10.5 g

Cholesterol: 84 mg; **Sodium:** 792 mg; **Potassium:** 841 mg

Vitamin A: 812%; **Vitamin C:** 24%; **Calcium:** 7%; **Iron:** 112%

Ingredients:

- ☐ 1 1/4 pounds beef stew meat, grass-fed
- ☐ 1/2 pounds mushrooms, sliced
- ☐ 2-3 sprigs fresh whole rosemary
- ☐ 2 tablespoons water
- ☐ 2 tablespoons Dijon mustard
- ☐ 2 tablespoon tapioca starch
- ☐ 2 large carrots, peeled, sliced
- ☐ 2 cups bone broth
- ☐ 2 cloves garlic, chopped
- ☐ 2 bay leaves
- ☐ 1/4 cup red wine vinegar
- ☐ 1 teaspoon Himalayan salt
- ☐ 1 teaspoon black pepper, freshly cracked
- ☐ 1 small (1 1/2 cups) rutabaga, peeled, diced
- ☐ 1 large onion, chopped
- ☐ Generous amount of ghee or coconut oil

Directions:

1. Pat the meat dry. Generously sprinkle with salt and pepper.
2. Heat the oil over high heat in a heavy skillet.

3. In a single layer, put the meat in the skillet, making sure each piece does not touch. Cook until all sides are brown. You may need in several batches so you don't overcrowd the skillet. When all sides are brown, transfer to a bowl to collect the juices. Set aside.
4. Lower the heat to medium. Add more grease into the pan if needed. Sauté the onion and the garlic, stirring often, until the onion is translucent.
5. Add the broth, Dijon mustard, wine vinegar. Bring to a simmer. Return the meat and the meat juice into the skillet. Stir and turn the heat off. Transfer to the cooker.
6. Add the rutabaga, carrots, mushrooms, bay leaves, and rosemary.
7. Cook for about 8 hours on low or for about 6 hours on high.
8. When the stew is cooked to your preference, ladle about 1 cup of the cooking liquid into a small saucepan. Bring to a boil.
9. Meanwhile, mix the water and the tapioca starch n a small bowl. Pour into the boiling cooking liquid. Cook for about 1 minute, constantly whisking, until thick.
10. Once the sauce is thick, pour into the cooker. Stir well to mix. Remove the bay leaves and the rosemary.
11. Serve immediately.

Applesauced Chicken

Prep Time: 10 minutes   **Cook Time:** Low for 7 hours

Slow Cooker: 3-4-quarts

Serving Size: 350 g   **Serves:** 4

Calories: 486

Total Fat: 16.9 g **Saturated Fat:** 4.6 g; **Trans Fat:** 0 g

Protein: 65.9 g

Total Carbs: 14.4 g; **Dietary Fibre:** 1.6 g; **Sugars:** 12.5 g

Net Carbs: 12.8 g

Cholesterol: 202 mg; **Sodium:** 198 mg; **Potassium:** 652mg

Vitamin A: 3%; **Vitamin C:** 3%; **Calcium:** 4%; **Iron:** 16%

Ingredients:
- 4 breasts (2 pounds) chicken, trimmed, cleaned
- 2 cups applesauce, organic, unsweetened
- 1/4 teaspoon black pepper
- 1/2 teaspoon onion powder
- 1/2 teaspoon garlic powder
- 1/4 teaspoon cinnamon

Directions:
1. Put the chicken in the slow cooker.
2. Add the applesauce and the rest of the ingredients.
3. Cover and cook.

Mustard-Honey Ham

Prep Time: 15 minutes	**Cook Time:** Low for 7 hours
Slow Cooker: 4-quarts	
Serving Size: 396 g	**Serves**: 6
Calories: 398	
Total Fat: 12.9 g **Saturated Fat**: 0.1 g; **Trans Fat**: 0 g	
Protein: 64 g	
Total Carbs: 6 g; **Dietary Fibre:** 0 g; **Sugars:** 2 g	
Net Carbs: 6 g	
Cholesterol: 155 mg; **Sodium:** 856 mg; **Potassium:** 842 mg	
Vitamin A: 0%; **Vitamin C:** 0%; **Calcium:** 2%; **Iron:** 13%	

Ingredients:

- 5 pounds (2.3 kg) fully cooked, bone-in ham
- 1/3 cup (75 ml) apple cider vinegar
- 1/2 cup (12 g) Splenda, reserve 2 tablespoons
- 1 tablespoon (11 g) brown mustard
- 1/2 teaspoon blackstrap molasses
- 1 teaspoon water

Directions:

1. Put the ham into the slow cooker.
2. In a mixing bowl, mix the reserved 2 tablespoon of Splenda and the vinegar together, making sure the sugar is dissolved. Pour the mix into the slow cooker.
3. In the same mixing bowl, mix the rest of the ingredients together. Spread the mix over the ham.
4. Cover the slow cooker and cook for about 7 hours on low.

Spicy Mexican Chicken

Prep Time: 15 minutes	**Cook Time:** Low for 6-7 hours

Slow Cooker: 3-4-quarts
Serving Size: 325 g   **Serves:** 4
Calories: 680
Total Fat: 52.3 g **Saturated Fat:** 6 g; **Trans Fat:** 0.2 g
Protein: 44 g
Total Carbs: 7.6 g; **Dietary Fibre:** 1.1 g; **Sugars:** 3.8 g
Net Carbs: 6.5 g
Cholesterol: 130 mg; **Sodium:** 811 mg; **Potassium:** 411 mg
Vitamin A: 21%; **Vitamin C:** 17%; **Calcium:** 6%; **Iron:** 15%

Ingredients:

- ☐ 1 jar (16 ounces) mild salsa
- ☐ 4 chicken breasts, skinless, cleaned, trimmed
- ☐ 1/4 teaspoon black pepper
- ☐ 1/3 cup water
- ☐ 1/2 teaspoon smoked paprika
- ☐ 1/2 teaspoon cumin
- ☐ 1/2 tablespoon dried oregano
- ☐ 1/2 tablespoon dried cilantro
- ☐ 1 teaspoon onion powder
- ☐ 1 teaspoon garlic powder
- ☐ 1 teaspoon chili powder
- ☐ 1 1/2 tablespoon dried parsley
- ☐ 3/4 cup canola oil

Directions:

1. Grease the cooker with the canola oil.
2. Put the chicken in the bottom of the cooker.
3. Add the water, salsa, and spices. Mix.
4. Close the lid and cook.

Yummy Pulled Pork

Prep Time: 5 minutes   **Cook Time:** Low for 8 hours

Slow Cooker: 3-4-quarts

Serving Size: 298 g   **Serves:** 6

Calories: 567

Total Fat: 31.9 g **Saturated Fat:** 12 g; **Trans Fat:** 0 g

Protein: 62.2 g

Total Carbs: 7.5 g; **Dietary Fibre:** 2.8 g; **Sugars:** 1.7 g

Net Carbs: 4.7 g

Cholesterol: 181 mg; **Sodium:** 598 mg; **Potassium:** 1036 mg

Vitamin A: 3%; **Vitamin C:** 21%; **Calcium:** 5%; **Iron:** 12%

Ingredients:
- 2 pounds pork loin
- 1/4 teaspoon chili powder
- 1/2 teaspoon paprika
- 1/2 teaspoon black pepper
- 1/2 cup lemon mixed with 12 packets low-carb sweetener
- 1/2 cup chicken or beef stock
- 1 teaspoon salt
- 1 teaspoon garlic powder
- 1 large onion, sliced
- 7/8 cup canola oil

Directions:
1. Grease the slow cooker with the oil.
2. Put the pork in the cooker. Cover with the stock.
3. Add the remaining ingredients.
4. Close the cooker lid and then cook.
5. When cooked, shred the meat according to your liking.

Poached Chicken and Vegetables

Prep Time: 10 minutes   **Cook Time:** Low for 8 hours

Slow Cooker: 6-quarts

Serving Size: 631 g   **Serves:** 4

Calories: 704

Total Fat: 13.5 g **Saturated Fat:** 3.8 g; **Trans Fat:** 0 g

Protein: 128 g

Total Carbs: 9.9 g; **Dietary Fibre:** 2.7 g; **Sugars**4.3 g

Net Carbs: 7.2 g

Cholesterol: 337mg; **Sodium:** 327 mg; **Potassium:** 1088 mg

Vitamin A: 108%; **Vitamin C:** 12%; **Calcium:** 10%; **Iron:** 25%

Ingredients:

- ☐ 1 piece 1-whole chicken, about 1 1/2 – 1 3/4 kg
- ☐ 2 carrots, sliced
- ☐ 2 onions, sliced
- ☐ 2 sticks celery, sliced
- ☐ 2 bay leaves
- ☐ 1/2 teaspoon dried tarragon
- ☐ 300 ml water

Directions:

1. Put all of the ingredients into the slow cooker. Cook for 8 hours on low.

Cheesy Chili

Prep Time: 10 minutes	**Cook Time:** Low for 7-8 hours

Slow Cooker: 3-quarts

Serving Size: 254 g   **Serves:** 6

Calories: 390

Total Fat: 18.3 g **Saturated Fat:** 1.6 g; **Trans Fat:** 0 g

Protein: 48.9g

Total Carbs: 6 g; **Dietary Fibre:** 1.2 g; **Sugars:** 2.5 g

Net Carbs: 5.6 g

Cholesterol: 152 mg; **Sodium:** 684 mg; **Potassium:** 645mg

Vitamin A: 17%; **Vitamin C**: 4%; **Calcium:** 17%; **Iron:** 14%

Ingredients:

- ☐ 2 pounds (900 g) chicken breasts, boneless, skinless
- ☐ 3 ounces (85 g) Monterey Jack cheese, shredded
- ☐ 1 jar (445 g or 16 ounces) salsa
- ☐ 1 tablespoon (8 g) chili powder
- ☐ 1 teaspoon chicken bouillon concentrate
- ☐ 6 tablespoons (90 g) light sour cream

Directions:

1. Put the chicken breasts into the slow cooker.
2. In a mixing bowl, stir the salsa, bouillon, and the chili powder together, making sure the bouillon is dissolved. Pour the mix over the breasts. Cover the slow cooker. Cook for about 7-8 hours on low.
3. When cooked, shred the chicken with a fork. Serve topped with the sour cream and the cheese.

Dinner

Tuna and Olive-Orange Tapenade

Prep Time: 60 minutes	**Cook Time:** Low for 15 minutes

Slow Cooker: 3-quarts

Serving Size: 266 g   **Serves:** 4

Calories: 414

Total Fat: 31 g **Saturated Fat:** 4.8 g; **Trans Fat:** 0 g

Protein: 25.1 g

Total Carbs: 9 g; **Dietary Fibre:** 3.6 g; **Sugars:** 0.9 g

Net Carbs: 5.4 g

Cholesterol: 26 mg; **Sodium:** 1044 mg; **Potassium:** 589 mg

Vitamin A: 88%; **Vitamin C:** 25%; **Calcium:** 13%; **Iron:** 27%

Ingredients:

- ☐ 12 ounces tuna (fresh center-cut), cut into thick steaks, thawed to room temperature
- ☐ 5 ounces (about 3/4 cup) brine-cured black olives, pitted
- ☐ 5 ounces (about 3/4 cup) mild green olives, pitted
- ☐ 5 tablespoons extra-virgin olive oil, plus more for the spinach
- ☐ 5- 6 ounces' fresh baby spinach
- ☐ 3 fresh bay leaves or 6 dried bay leaves
- ☐ 2 cloves garlic, thinly sliced
- ☐ 1/4 cup vegetable broth or fish stock
- ☐ 1/4 cup dry white or rose wine
- ☐ 1/2 teaspoon kosher salt, plus more as needed
- ☐ 1/2 medium onion, finely chopped
- ☐ 1 teaspoon red or white wine vinegar
- ☐ 1 orange zest
- ☐ Freshly ground black pepper

Directions:

1. In the slow cooker, combine the broth, wine, the 4 tablespoons canola oil, bay leaves, and salt. Season with pepper to taste. Stir to combine. Cover the slow cooker with lid. Cook for 30 minutes on low.

2. Add in the tuna. Turn to coat each piece evenly with the cooked broth wine mix. Cover and cook for 25-35 minutes on low or until the fish is opaque. When the fish is opaque, remove with slotted spoon and transfer to a serving platter. Using two forks, shred the fish into large flakes. Cover with foil to keep warm. Discard the cooking liquid.

3. While the fish is cooking, put the orange zest, garlic, olives, vinegar, and the remaining 1 tablespoon of canola oil in a food processor. Pulse until the mix is a thick puree.

4. When ready to serve, put the spinach in a mixing bowl. Toss with a little canola oil. Season with salt and pepper. Divide into the number of servings indicated, creating a bed for the tuna. Evenly distribute the tuna flakes into the number of servings. Top with the tapenade. Serve at room temperature.

Slow Leg Lamb

Prep Time: 10 minutes   **Cook Time:** Low for 8 hours

Slow Cooker: 3-quarts

Serving Size: 204 g   **Serves:** 4

Calories: 471

Total Fat: 34.2 g **Saturated Fat:** 26 g; **Trans Fat:** 0 g

Protein: 25.8 g

Total Carbs: 6.6 g; **Dietary Fibre:** 2.7 g; **Sugars:** 0.5 g

Net Carbs: 3.9 g

Cholesterol: 79 mg; **Sodium:** 369 mg; **Potassium:** 498 mg

Vitamin A: 20%; **Vitamin C:** 10%; **Calcium:** 10%; **Iron:** 32%

Ingredients:
- 1 cup fresh mint, chopped
- 1 cup white wine
- 1 lamb leg, shank removed
- 1/2 teaspoon salt
- 3 sprigs rosemary, chopped
- 6 garlic cloves, minced
- 8 tablespoon coconut oil, divided
- Fresh black pepper

Directions:
1. In a bowl, mix 1 tablespoon coconut and the herbs, creating a paste.
2. In a large skillet over medium-high heat, heat the remaining coconut oil; sear all the sides of the lamb leg.
3. Rub the paste all over the lamb leg, place in the cooker. Pour the wine and the coconut oil from the skillet around the lamb; cover and cook for 8 hours on low.

Buttery Tilapia

Prep Time: 10 minutes	**Cook Time:** High for 2 hours

Slow Cooker: 4-quarts

Serving Size: 155 g	**Serves**: 4

Calories: 309

Total Fat: 24.1 g **Saturated Fat**: 15.1 g; **Trans Fat**: 0 g

Protein: 21.9 g

Total Carbs: 2.5 g; **Dietary Fibre:** 0 g; **Sugars:** 0 g

Net Carbs: 2.5 g

Cholesterol: 116 mg; **Sodium:** 209 mg; **Potassium:** 73mg

Vitamin A: 27%; **Vitamin C**: 20%; **Calcium**: 5%; **Iron**: 10%

Ingredients:
- ☐ 4 tilapia fillets

For the garlic-butter compound:
- ☐ 8 tablespoons butter
- ☐ 8 garlic cloves
- ☐ 8 teaspoons parsley, chopped

Directions:
1. In a large mixing bowl, mix all of the garlic-butter compound ingredients.
2. Place each tilapia fillet in the middle of a large sheet of aluminum foil. Generously season fillets with salt and pepper. Divide the garlic butter compound into each fillet. Wrap the foil around the fish, sealing all sides. Place into the slow cooker. Cover with lid. Cook for 2 hours on high.

Creamy Turkey and Mushrooms

Prep Time: 15 minutes	**Cook Time:** Low for 2-3 hours

Slow Cooker: 6-quarts

Serving Size: 322 g **Serves:** 4

Calories: 345

Total Fat: 14.4 g **Saturated Fat:** 6.4 g; **Trans Fat:** 0 g

Protein: 38.7 g

Total Carbs: 14 g; **Dietary Fibre:** 0.8 g; **Sugars:** 11 g

Net Carbs: 13.2 g

Cholesterol: 106 mg; **Sodium:** 594 mg; **Potassium:** 753mg

Vitamin A: 9%; **Vitamin C**: 25%; **Calcium**: 25%; **Iron**: 66%

Ingredients:

- ☐ 4 ounces mushrooms, stems and pieces
- ☐ 3 cup turkey, cooked and cubed
- ☐ 13 ounces can evaporated milk, drained
- ☐ 10 ounces can cream of mushroom soup
- ☐ 1/8 teaspoon pepper
- ☐ 1/4 cup pimento, chopped
- ☐ 1/4 cup onion, finely chopped
- ☐ 1/4 cup green pepper, finely chopped
- ☐ 1/4 cup celery, finely chopped
- ☐ 1/2 teaspoon seasoned salt

Directions:

1. Put all of the ingredients into the slow cooker. Cover with lid. Cook for 2–3 hours on low or until heated through, stirring once while cooking.

Meatballs on Spaghetti Squash

Prep Time: 20 minutes	**Cook Time:** Low for 5 hours, high for 3 hours

Slow Cooker: 6-quarts
Serving Size: 270 g   **Serves:** 4
Calories: 495
Total Fat: 40.3 g **Saturated Fat:** 11.5 g; **Trans Fat:** 0.3 g
Protein: 23.9 g
Total Carbs: 10 g; **Dietary Fibre:** 1.6 g; **Sugars:** 4.5 g
Net Carbs: 8.4 g
Cholesterol: 97 mg; **Sodium:** 1378 mg; **Potassium:** 727 mg
Vitamin A: 8%; **Vitamin C:** 17%; **Calcium:** 5%; **Iron:** 15%

Ingredients:
- ☐ 1 pound ground Italian sausage
- ☐ 1 can (14 ounces) tomato sauce
- ☐ 1 medium spaghetti squash
- ☐ 2 tablespoons canola oil
- ☐ 4-6 cloves garlic, whole
- ☐ 2 teaspoons Italian seasoning (basil, oregano, thyme), to taste

Optional:
- ☐ 2 tablespoons hot pepper relish
- ☐ Parsley, for garnishing

Directions:
1. Put the tomato sauce, garlic, canola oil, Italian seasoning, and the hot pepper relish (if using) into the cooker.
2. Cut the squash in half. Scoop the seeds out.
3. With the meat side down, place the 2 squash halves into the cooker.
4. Roll the ground sausage into meatballs. Fit as many meatballs as you can in the sauce around the squash.
5. Cook for about 5 hours on low or for about 3 hours on high.
6. With a fork, pull the spaghetti out of the squash. Top with the sauce and the meatballs.

7. Garnish with parsley if desired.

Easy Mexicana Chicken

Prep Time: 5 minutes	**Cook Time:** Low for 6-8 hours, high for 4 hours

Slow Cooker: 3-quarts

Serving Size: 136 g   **Serves:** 10 (1/2 cup each)

Calories: 318

Total Fat: 24.6 g **Saturated Fat:** 3 g; **Trans Fat:** 0.1 g

Protein: 20.8 g

Total Carbs: 3.4 g; **Dietary Fibre:** 0.7 g; **Sugars:** 1.4 g

Net Carbs: 2.7 g

Cholesterol: 62 mg; **Sodium:** 347 mg; **Potassium:** 6310mg

Vitamin A: 4%; **Vitamin C:** 2%; **Calcium:** 3%; **Iron:** 6%

Ingredients:

- ☐ 1 1/2 pounds chicken breasts
- ☐ 1 jar (16 ounce) salsa
- ☐ 1 packet (1 1/4 ounce) taco seasoning, low-sodium
- ☐ 7/8 canola oil

For serving:

- ☐ Chopped tomatoes
- ☐ Shredded cheese
- ☐ Black beans
- ☐ Corn
- ☐ Guacamole or chopped avocados
- ☐ Sour cream
- ☐ Hot sauce

Directions:

1. Pour the chicken in the bottom of the slow cooker.
2. Sprinkle with taco seasoning. Pour the salsa and the oil over the top.
3. Cook for 6-8 hours on ow or for 4 hours on high.

4. When cooked, shred the chicken using 2 forks. Stir to combine with the salsa. Serve with desired toppings.

Perfect Roast Chicken

Prep Time: 5 minutes	**Cook Time:** High for 4 hours

Slow Cooker: 4-6-quarts

Serving Size: 510 g	**Serves:** 6

Calories: 839

Total Fat: 33.9 g **Saturated Fat:** 9.3 g; **Trans Fat:** 0 g

Protein: 132.3 g

Total Carbs: 7.3 g; **Dietary Fibre:** 1.9 g; **Sugars:** 2.2 g

Net Carbs: 5.4 g

Cholesterol: 404 mg; **Sodium:** 1031 mg; **Potassium:** 1263 mg

Vitamin A: 85%; **Vitamin C:** 17%; **Calcium:** 10%; **Iron:** 36%

Equipment:
- ☐ 8 inches kitchen twine

Ingredients:
- ☐ 4-6 pounds whole chicken, giblets removed
- ☐ 2 tired old carrots, celery, or parsnips
- ☐ 2 teaspoons sea salt
- ☐ 2 teaspoons pepper
- ☐ 1 yellow onion, cut into quarters
- ☐ 1 teaspoon dried thyme
- ☐ 1 tablespoon paprika
- ☐ 1 lemon or an orange, cut into quarters

Optional:
- ☐ 1 head garlic, cut crosswise into halves

Directions:
1. In a small mixing bowl, combine the thyme, salt, and pepper.
2. Put the carrots, celery, or parsnips into the bottom of the cooker, making a vegetable roasting rack.
3. Sprinkle the inside cavity of the chicken with 1/2 of the thyme mixture. Put 1 half of the garlic head, 2 quarters of the onion, and 1 quarter of the lemon into the cavity

4. Then plug in the remaining ingredients into the cavity, positioning the lemon with the rind side out. The lemon will act as a plug.
5. Place the chicken in the cooker.
6. Tie the legs so that the vegetables in the cavity stays in place.
7. Sprinkle the remaining 1/2 of the thyme mixture over the chicken.
8. Sprinkle the chicken top with the paprika.
9. Close the cooker lid and cook.

Mushroom Stroganoff

Prep Time: 15 minutes	**Cook Time:** High for 4 hours	
Slow Cooker: 3-quarts		
Serving Size: 445 g	**Serves**: 3	
Calories: 151		
Total Fat: 8.6 g **Saturated Fat:** 4.7 g; **Trans Fat:** 0 g		
Protein: 7.7 g		
Total Carbs: 14.2g; **Dietary Fibre:** 3.7 g; **Sugars:** 4.7 g		
Net Carbs: 10.5 g		
Cholesterol: 17 mg; **Sodium:** 811 mg; **Potassium:** 775mg		
Vitamin A: 45%; **Vitamin C:** 41%; **Calcium:** 7%; **Iron:** 34%		

Ingredients:

- ☐ 600 ml chicken stock
- ☐ 500 g mushrooms, sliced
- ☐ 4 tablespoons sour cream, heaped
- ☐ 3 teaspoons paprika
- ☐ 3 cloves garlic, thinly sliced
- ☐ 1 tablespoon tomato ketchup
- ☐ 1 tablespoon butter
- ☐ 1 onion, diced
- ☐ Handful fresh parsley, chopped

Optional:

- ☐ Spaghetti squash or zucchini pasta, hot cooked

Directions:

1. In a large pan, melt the butter. Add the onion and mushroom. Gently cook for about 5-10 minutes or until the onions are softened slightly and the mushrooms are starting to shrink, but not fully cooked. Transfer into the slow cooker.
2. Pour in the stock. Add in the ketchup, the garlic, and the paprika. Cover and cook for 4 hours on high.

3. When cooked, stir in the sour cream and the chopped parsley
4. Serve over hot cooked spaghetti squash or zucchini pasta, if desired.

Mashed Cauliflower

Prep Time: 15 minutes	**Cook Time:** Low for 6-8 hours, high for 3-4 hours

Slow Cooker: 4-quarts

Serving Size: 474 g   **Serves:** 6

Calories: 105

Total Fat: 4.6 g **Saturated Fat:** 4 g; **Trans Fat:** 0 g

Protein: 5.2 g

Total Carbs: 14.5 g; **Dietary Fibre:** 6.1 g; **Sugars:** 5.5 g

Net Carbs: 8.4 g

Cholesterol: 11 mg; **Sodium**: 81 mg; **Potassium**: 790 mg

Vitamin A: 6%; **Vitamin C**: 179%; **Calcium**: 11%; **Iron**: 13%

Ingredients:
- ☐ 1 large head (about 3 pounds) cauliflower
- ☐ 1 small package fresh dill (about 1/3 cup chopped)
- ☐ 6 cloves garlic
- ☐ Splash of coconut milk (or 1-2tablespoons of ghee or butter)
- ☐ Salt and pepper, to taste
- ☐ About 6 cups water, or more

Directions:
1. Remove the base stem and the leaves of the cauliflower. Cut into florets. Put them into the cooker.
2. Add 1/2 of the dill and the garlic into the cooker.
3. Add enough water to cover the cauliflower.
4. Cover and cook for about 6-8 hours on low or about 4-5 hours on high.
5. Wearing heavy-duty oven mitts, carefully drain the cooker into a colander. Or you can wait for the cooker to cool. Remove the cooked dill. Transfer the cauliflower and the garlic into a bowl.
6. Add a pinch of salt and pepper. Add the remaining fresh dill (stems removed) and coconut milk or your butter of your choice. Puree with an immersion blender.
7. Garnish with more fresh dill sprigs.

Notes:
If you don't have an immersion blender, add everything into a food processor.

Chicken Cacciatore II

Prep Time: 20 minutes	**Cook Time:** Low for 8 hours; high for 4 hours

Slow Cooker: 3-quarts
Serving Size: 246 g   **Serves**: 4
Calories: 375
Total Fat: 10 g **Saturated Fat**: 1.6 g; **Trans Fat**: 0 g
Protein: 48.9g
Total Carbs: 6 g; **Dietary Fibre**: 3.8 g; **Sugars**: 6.6 g
Net Carbs: 6.2 g
Cholesterol: 96 mg; **Sodium**: 284 mg; **Potassium**: 312 mg
Vitamin A: 31%; **Vitamin C**: 45%; **Calcium**: 7%; **Iron**: 17%

Ingredients:

- [ ] 28 ounces canned crushed tomatoes
- [ ] 8 chicken thighs, skins removed, with bones
- [ ] 1 bay leaf
- [ ] 1 teaspoon dried oregano
- [ ] 1/2 green bell pepper, sliced into strips
- [ ] 1/2 large onion, sliced
- [ ] 1/2 red bell pepper, sliced into strips
- [ ] 1/2 cup canola oil, divided

To taste:
- [ ] Salt & Fresh pepper

For topping:
- [ ] 1/4 cup fresh herbs (basil or parsley)

Directions:

1. Over medium-high, grease a large skillet with 1/2 cup of the oil. Cook and brown each side of the chicken. Season with salt and pepper. Put into the slow cooker with the oils.
2. Into the same skillet add the remaining 1/2 cup canola oil. Add in the onions and the peppers. Sauté until the juices are released and turn golden. Add into the slow cooker.
3. Add the tomatoes into the slow cooker. Add in the bay leaf, oregano, salt, and pepper. Stir. Cover with lid. Cook for 8 hours on low or for 4 hours on high. When cooked, remove bay leaf. Adjust salt and pepper according to taste.

Mediterranean-Style Beef Stew

Prep Time: 30-45 minutes	**Cook Time:** Low for 6-8 hours, high for 3-4 hours

Slow Cooker: 2 1/2 or 3 1/2-quarts

Serving Size: 326 g   **Serves:** 8

Calories: 644

Total Fat: 51.6 g **Saturated Fat:** 8.7 g; **Trans Fat:** 0.1 g

Protein: 37.6 g

Total Carbs: 7.5 g; **Dietary Fibre:** 2.6 g; **Sugars:** 3.4 g

Net Carbs: 4.9 g

Cholesterol: 120 mg; **Sodium:** 541 mg; **Potassium:** 643 mg

Vitamin A: 14%; **Vitamin C:** 21%; **Calcium:** 6%; **Iron:** 36%

Ingredients:

- ☐ 2 pounds chuck steak, trimmed, cut into bite-sized pieces
- ☐ 8 ounces mushrooms, sliced
- ☐ 1 can (14 1/2 ounces) diced tomatoes with juice
- ☐ 1 can black olives, cut in halves or quarters
- ☐ 1 cup beef stock
- ☐ 1 onion, diced in 1/2 inch pieces
- ☐ 1 tablespoon capers, (or more)
- ☐ 1/2 cup tomato sauce
- ☐ 1/4 cup balsamic vinegar
- ☐ 1-2 tablespoons canola oil
- ☐ 2 tablespoons fresh parsley, finely chopped (or 1 tablespoon dried parsley)
- ☐ 2 tablespoons fresh rosemary, finely chopped (or 1 tablespoon dried cracked rosemary)
- ☐ Fresh ground black pepper, to taste
- ☐ Salt, to taste

Optional:

- ☐ 1/2 cup garlic cloves, cut into thin slices

Directions:

1. In a heavy frying pan, pour 1/2 cup of canola oil. Add the mushrooms. Sauté for several minutes until starting to brown. Put the mushrooms in the cooker with the oil.
2. Add 1/4 cup oil in the pan and sauté the onions for 5 minutes until starting to brown. Add to the cooker.
3. Add the remaining 1/2 cup oil. Add the diced beef. Cook for about 10-15 minutes or until brown. Add to the cooker.
4. Pour the beef stock in the pan. Simmer for a few minutes, scraping the browned bits and until slightly reduced. Add to the cooker.
5. Except for the salt and the black pepper, add the remaining ingredients into the cooker. Stir gently to combine.
6. Cover and cook for about 6-8 hours on low or about 3-4 hours on high.
7. When cooked, season with salt and pepper.
8. Serve hot.

Gravy-licious Roast Chicken

Prep Time: 20 minutes	**Cook Time:** Low for 4-6 hours

Slow Cooker: 3-quarts

Serving Size: 266 g   **Serves:** 10

Calories: 382

Total Fat: 9.5 g **Saturated Fat:** 3.5 g; **Trans Fat:** 0 g

Protein: 66.1 g

Total Carbs: 3.1 g; **Dietary Fibre:** 0.6 g; **Sugars:** 1.1 g

Net Carbs: 2.5 g

Cholesterol: 181 mg; **Sodium:** 180 mg; **Potassium:** 477mg

Vitamin A: 3%; **Vitamin C:** 4%; **Calcium:** 4%; **Iron:** 12%

Ingredients:

- ☐ 6 garlic cloves, peeled
- ☐ 4-5 pounds chicken, organic kosher
- ☐ 2 tablespoons ghee
- ☐ 2 onions, chopped medium
- ☐ 1/4 cup white wine or extra chicken stock
- ☐ 1/4 cup chicken stock
- ☐ 1 teaspoon tomato paste (or up to 1 tablespoon)
- ☐ Freshly ground pepper
- ☐ Kosher salt
- ☐ Sunny Paris seasoning (or your preferred seasoning)

Directions:

1. In a large cast-iron over medium heat, melt the ghee. Put in the onions and the garlic. Add in the tomato paste. Cook for about 8-10 until soft and lightly browned.
2. Pour in the wine to deglaze the pan. Transfer the mixture into the slow cooker.
3. Dry the chicken. Season well on both the inside and outside with the salt, pepper, and your preferred seasoning. With the breast down, put the chicken into the slow cooker. Close the

lid. Cook for about 4-6 hours on low. When cooked, transfer the chicken into a serving plate. Let rest for 20 minutes.

4. Defat the cooking liquid. Adjust the seasoning. Blend with an immersion blender. Serve with the chicken.

Chinese Style Spare Ribs

Prep Time: 20 minutes, plus 12-24 hours   **Cook Time:** High for 4-6 hours

Slow Cooker: 4-6-quarts

Serving Size: 834 g   **Serves:** 4

Calories: 1302

Total Fat: 80.4 g **Saturated Fat:** 28.6 g; **Trans Fat:** 0.7 g

Protein: 121.6 g

Total Carbs: 3.1 g; **Dietary Fibre:** 0 g; **Sugars:** 1.2 g

Net Carbs: 3.1 g

Cholesterol: 467 mg; **Sodium:** 1559 mg; **Potassium:** 1513mg

Vitamin A: 1%; **Vitamin C:** 0%; **Calcium:** 18%; **Iron:** 38%

Ingredients:

- 3-4 pounds pork ribs, pasture-raised
- 1 teaspoon sea salt
- 1-2 cups water
- 2 tablespoons rice wine vinegar (or raw apple cider vinegar)
- 2-4 cups white vinegar
- 3 tablespoons coconut aminos (or wheat-free tamari)
- Chinese 5-spice powder, to taste
- Garlic powder, to taste
- Ground black pepper, to taste
- Sea salt, to taste

Directions:

1. Cover your ribs with a mixture of white vinegar and water in a 2:1 ratio. Mix in 1 teaspoon sea salt. Soak for 12 hours or overnight. Keep the container in the refrigerator.
2. When ready to cook, drain the ribs thoroughly.
3. Sprinkle every side with a generous amount of salt, garlic powder, and black pepper.
4. Heavily coat every side with the 5-spice powder until the meat appears covered with dark orange powder.
5. Place the ribs upright in the cooker.

6. Add the coconut aminos and the rice wine into the bottom of the slow cooker.
7. Cook for about 4-6 hours on high.
8. Carefully watch the liquid in the pot.

Boeuf Bourguignon

Prep Time: 30 minutes	**Cook Time:** Low for 8 hours; high for 6 hours

Slow Cooker: 6-quarts

Serving Size: 329 g   **Serves**: 8

Calories: 517

Total Fat: 21.2 g **Saturated Fat:** 6.7 g; **Trans Fat:** 0 g

Protein: 58.2 g

Total Carbs: 9.2 g; **Dietary Fibre:** 1.7 g; **Sugars:** 3.6 g

Net Carbs: 7.5 g

Cholesterol: 147 mg; **Sodium:** 1157 mg; **Potassium:** 814mg

Vitamin A: 1%; **Vitamin C:** 9%; **Calcium:** 4%; **Iron:** 33%

Ingredients:

- ☐ 1 bay leaf
- ☐ 1 large onion, thinly sliced
- ☐ 1 tablespoon oil
- ☐ 150 g mushrooms
- ☐ 1 kg steak, cut into 2 1/2 cm cubes
- ☐ 2 cloves garlic, crushed to a paste with 1 teaspoon salt
- ☐ 2 teaspoons dried thyme
- ☐ 200 ml stock
- ☐ 250 g bacon, thick-cut, cut into lardons
- ☐ 350 g small onions, peeled, whole
- ☐ 500 ml Burgundy wine

Directions:

1. In a large skillet, cook the meat until browned. When browned, transfer into the slow cooker.
2. Sauté the onions until soft and transfer into the slow cooker.
3. Lightly fry the bacon and then transfer into the slow cooker.
4. Cook for 8 hours on low or for 6 hours on high.

5. When cooked, serve with a generous amount of your favorite
   green   salad

Low-Carb Slow Paella

Prep Time: 30 minutes	**Cook Time:** Low for 6 hours plus high for 30 minutes

Slow Cooker: 6-quarts
Serving Size: 299 g   **Serves:** 8
Calories: 332
Total Fat: 11.6 g **Saturated Fat:** 2.2 g; **Trans Fat:** 0 g
Protein: 48 g
Total Carbs: 6.5 g; **Dietary Fibre:** 2.1 g; **Sugars:** 3.1 g
Net Carbs: 4.4 g
Cholesterol: 150 mg; **Sodium:** 440mg; **Potassium:** 594 mg
Vitamin A: 18%; **Vitamin C:** 64%; **Calcium:** 6%; **Iron:** 11%

Ingredients:

- ☐ 6 ounces shrimp
- ☐ 6 ounces diced ham or chorizo links
- ☐ 6 chicken legs (about 3 pounds)
- ☐ 1 can (14 1/2 ounces) tomato wedges, drained
- ☐ 1/4 cup canola oil
- ☐ 1/2 teaspoon saffron threads
- ☐ 1/2 cup snow pea pods, fresh, cut into 1/2-inch pieces
- ☐ 1 teaspoon chicken bouillon concentrate
- ☐ 1 head cauliflower
- ☐ 1 green bell pepper
- ☐ 1 cup (235 ml) chicken broth
- ☐ 1 cup (160 g) onion, chopped
- ☐ 1 clove garlic, crushed

Directions:

1. In a large skillet, brown the chicken in the canola oil.
2. While the chicken is cooking, put in the garlic, onion, and green pepper into the slow cooker.

3. When the chicken is browned, transfer into the slow cooker. If using chorizo, brown in the same skillet. When cooked, transfer into the slow cooker. If using ham, simply put it directly into the cooker.

4. Put the tomatoes over the meat ingredients.

5. In a mixing bowl, mix the broth, bouillon, and the saffron together. Pour into the slow cooker. Cover. Cook for 6 hours on low.

6. After 6 hours, turn the heat to high. Add in the peas and the shrimps. Re-cover. Cook for 30 minutes on high.

7. Meanwhile, shred the cauliflower in a food processor. When shredded, put in a microwavable casserole dish with a lid. Add 45-60 ml water into the dish. Microwave for about 8-9 minutes on high. Serve together with the paella.

Slow Roasted Lamb

Prep Time: 10 minutes **Cook Time:** Low for 7 hours	
Slow Cooker: 3-4-quarts	
Serving Size: 383 g **Serves:** 6	
Calories: 355	
Total Fat: 11.9 g **Saturated Fat:** 4 g; **Trans Fat:** 0 g	
Protein: 44.4 g	
Total Carbs: 14.5 g; **Dietary Fibre:** 3.4 g; **Sugars:** 8.2 g	
Net Carbs: 11.1 g	
Cholesterol: 136 mg; **Sodium:** 431 mg; **Potassium:** 907 mg	
Vitamin A: 85%; **Vitamin C:** 23%; **Calcium:** 5%; **Iron:** 28%	

Ingredients:

- [ ] 2 pounds lamb roast
- [ ] 2 cans (8 ounces) diced green chilies
- [ ] 1 teaspoon garlic powder
- [ ] 1 teaspoon chili powder
- [ ] 1 tablespoon paprika
- [ ] 1 tablespoon cumin
- [ ] 1 package frozen diced bell peppers
- [ ] 1 can (14 1/2 ounces) fired-roasted diced tomatoes
- [ ] Salt and pepper to taste

Directions:

1. Place the lamb in the cooker.
2. Pour all the vegetables in, and then all of the spices. Stir well to evenly combine the vegetables and the spices.
3. Cook for about 7 hours on low.
4. Shred the lamb with a fork. Serve.

Pork Ramen

Prep Time: 10 minutes   **Cook Time:** Low for 7 hours, plus 5-10 minutes

Slow Cooker: 3-4-quarts

Serving Size: 483 g   **Serves:** 6

Calories: 635

Total Fat: 41.8 g **Saturated Fat:** 15.2 g; **Trans Fat:** 0 g

Protein: 50.8 g

Total Carbs: 10.5 g; **Dietary Fibre:** 2.3 g; **Sugars:** 4.3 g

Net Carbs: 8.2 g

Cholesterol: 170 mg; **Sodium:** 3224 mg; **Potassium:** 1139 mg

Vitamin A: 9%; **Vitamin C:** 21%; **Calcium:** 9%; **Iron:** 25%

Ingredients:
- 2 1/2 pounds pork shoulder
- 4 cups chicken broth
- 2 tablespoons chili garlic sauce*
- 2 cups baby portabellas, sliced
- 1/4 cup rice vinegar
- 1/4 cup fish sauce
- 1/2 cup coconut aminos or tamari
- 1 zucchini, spiralized
- 1 teaspoon sea salt
- 1 teaspoon black pepper
- 1 tablespoons fresh ginger
- 1 tablespoons Chinese 5-spice, see blend below
- 1 lime, juiced

For serving:
- 1 large bunch cilantro
- 2 jalapeños, sliced

5-spice blend:
- 1 teaspoon lemon pepper
- 1 teaspoon cinnamon
- 1/2 teaspoon fennel seeds

☐   1 teaspoon star anise seeds
☐   1/4 teaspoon clove

Directions:
1. Place the pork in the bottom of the cooker.
2. Except for the zoodles, mushrooms, salt, and pepper, pour all of the ingredients on top of the pork.
3. Cover and cook.
4. When the 7 hours is almost done, spiralize the zucchini and slice the mushrooms.
5. After 7 hours, remove the pork from the cooker. Shred the meat using 2 forks.
6. Skim the fat off the broth, if desired.
7. Return the pork to the cooker. Put in the zoodles and the mushrooms.
8. Season with salt and pepper.
9. Cook for about 5-10 minutes or until the mushrooms are soft.
10. Serve with a handful of cilantros and sliced jalapeños.

Veggie Beef Stew

Prep Time: 10 minutes	**Cook Time:** Low for 8 hours

Slow Cooker: 3-4-quarts

Serving Size: 433 g **Serves:** 4

Calories: 473

Total Fat: 14.8 g **Saturated Fat**: 5.5 g; **Trans Fat**: 0 g

Protein: 71.5 g

Total Carbs: 9.6 g; **Dietary Fibre:** 2.9 g; **Sugars:** 3.3 g

Net Carbs: 6.7 g

Cholesterol: 203 mg; **Sodium:** 866 mg; **Potassium:** 1242mg

Vitamin A: 141%; **Vitamin C:** 12%; **Calcium:** 5%; **Iron:** 245%

Ingredients:
- ☐ 3 bay leaves
- ☐ 2 stalks celery, roughly chopped
- ☐ 2 pounds stewing beef, pastured
- ☐ 2 large carrots, peeled, chopped
- ☐ 2 cups beef or chicken stock (or 1 cup beer or wine and 1 cup stock)
- ☐ 1/8 cup arrowroot powder, for thickening
- ☐ 1/2 teaspoon salt
- ☐ 1/2 teaspoon black pepper
- ☐ 1 teaspoon oregano
- ☐ 1 teaspoon dried rosemary
- ☐ 1 teaspoon basil
- ☐ 1 tablespoons paprika
- ☐ 1 tablespoon balsamic vinegar
- ☐ medium onion, chopped
- ☐ 1-3 cloves garlic, minced

Directions:
1. Put the meat into the cooker.
2. Pour the liquid ingredients into the cooker.
3. Except for the arrowroot powder, add the remaining of the ingredients.

4. Cover and cook.

To thicken:

1. Before serving, spoon most of the liquid with a ladle, transferring into a small saucepan. Bring to a boil.
2. In a small bowl, ladle a small amount of the liquid and then sprinkle the arrowroot, whisking as you add. Mix until there are no more lumps.
3. Slowly pour the arrowroot mixture into the saucepan. Remove from heat and continue whisking. Do not reheat the liquid because this will break the thickener bond.
4. If the liquid is not thick enough, put some water and arrowroot flour in the small bowl. Whisk to mix and then slowly add into the gravy in the saucepan.
5. Pour the gravy back into the cooker. Stir gently and then serve.

Moroccan Lamb

Prep Time: 10 minutes	**Cook Time:** 8 hours

Slow Cooker: 3-4-quarts

Serving Size: 344 g   **Serves:** 5-6

Calories: 383

Total Fat: 24.2 g **Saturated Fat:** 9.5 g; **Trans Fat:** 0 g

Protein: 54

Total Carbs: 12.5 g; **Dietary Fibre:** 4.2 g; **Sugars:** 9.1 g

Net Carbs: 8.3 g

Cholesterol: 183 mg; **Sodium:** 316 mg; **Potassium:** 763mg

Vitamin A: 51%; **Vitamin C:** 71%; **Calcium:** 7%; **Iron:** 32%

Ingredients:
- ☐ 2 pound lamb (cuts of choice), diced
- ☐ 1 can crushed tomatoes
- ☐ 1 cup apricots, diced
- ☐ 1 red bell pepper, diced
- ☐ 2 daikon, peeled, diced
- ☐ 3 tablespoons ghee or clarified butter
- ☐ 4 tablespoons Ras El Hanout spice blend (or ground coriander)

Directions:
1. Put the spice blend in a dry, hot frying pan. Roast it for a couple minutes.
2. Add the diced lamb into the frying pan. Stir until all the pieces are evenly coated with the spices.
3. Add the ghee and quickly sear the meat.
4. Put the seared meat into the cooker. Add the remaining ingredients and then cook.
5. Serve over Cauliflower Tabbouleh – see below

Cauliflower Tabbouleh

Prep Time: 20-30 minutes   **Cook Time:** 0 minutes

Serving Size: 209 g   **Serves:** 6

Calories: 148

Total Fat: 12.5 g **Saturated Fat:** 1 g; **Trans Fat:** 0.1 g

Protein: 2.6 g

Total Carbs: 8.7 g; **Dietary Fibre:** 3.1 g; **Sugars:** 4.3 g

Net Carbs: 5.6 g

Cholesterol: 0 mg; **Sodium:** 186 mg; **Potassium:** 480 mg

Vitamin A: 22%; **Vitamin C:** 88%; **Calcium:** 4%; **Iron:** 7%

Ingredients:

- ☐ 1/2 large head cauliflower, tough core discarded, chopped into florets
- ☐ 3 tablespoons lemon juice, freshly squeezed, plus more to taste
- ☐ 3 large bunches flat-leaf parsley, finely chopped
- ☐ 2 tablespoons fresh mint, finely chopped, plus more to taste
- ☐ 2 cups tomatoes, finely diced (about 8 large tomatoes, flesh scooped out)
- ☐ 1/3 cup extra-virgin canola oil, cold-pressed, plus more to taste
- ☐ 1/2 teaspoon sea salt, plus more to taste
- ☐ 1 English cucumber, peeled, seeds scooped out, finely diced
- ☐ 1 bunch green onions, finely chopped (green and white parts)
- ☐ Cracked pepper, to taste

Directions:

1. Put the cauliflower florets into a food processor with the S blade. Pulse for a few minutes until the florets are couscous consistency.
2. Transfer to a large mixing bowl. Combine with the remaining ingredients.

3. Add more salt, pepper, canola oil, lemon juice, or mint to your taste.

Beef Tongue with Roasted Pepper Sauce

Prep Time: 10 minutes   **Cook Time:** Low for 8 hours

Slow Cooker: 2-3-quarts

Serving Size: 298 g   **Serves:** 6

Calories: 190

Total Fat: 10.1 g **Saturated Fat:** 3.6 g; **Trans Fat:** 0.4 g

Protein: 11.2 g

Total Carbs: 15.3 g; **Dietary Fibre:** 3.8 g; **Sugars:** 8.1 g

Net Carbs: 11.5 g

Cholesterol: 57 mg; **Sodium:** 94 mg; **Potassium:** 690 mg

Vitamin A: 34%; **Vitamin C:** 75%; **Calcium:** 5%; **Iron:** 18%

Ingredients:
For the tongue:
- [ ] 1 beef tongue
- [ ] 3 garlic cloves, crushed
- [ ] 3 bay leaves
- [ ] 1 onion, sliced
- [ ] Water, to cover tongue
- [ ] Sea salt and pepper

For the sauce:
- [ ] 6 ounces tomato paste
- [ ] 3 garlic cloves, minced
- [ ] 20 ounces tomatoes, sliced
- [ ] 1 teaspoon thyme
- [ ] 1 teaspoon oregano
- [ ] 1 roasted serrano chili pepper, diced
- [ ] 1 roasted red pepper, peeled and diced
- [ ] 1 onion, diced
- [ ] Salt and pepper, to taste

Directions:
For the tongue:
1. Wash the beef tongue under cold water and then pat dry.

2. Line the bottom of the cooker with the garlic, onion, and bay leaves.
3. Lay the tongue on top. Generously season with the salt and pepper.
4. Add as much water as needed to submerge the tongue completely.
5. Cover and cook for about 8 hours on low.
6. When cooked, remove the tongue from the cooker. Remove the skin and shred. Serve with the sauce below.

For the sauce:
1. In a saucepan over medium heat, sauté the garlic, onions, serrano chili, and red pepper until the onions are translucent.
2. Add the remaining ingredients. Stir well.
3. Reduce the heat to low. Simmer for about 30 minutes.
4. You can leave the sauce chunky as it is. If you want a smoother consistency, blend it.
5. Serve on the shredded tongue.

Corned Beef with Cabbage

Prep Time: 30 minutes   **Cook Time:** Low for 7 hours

Slow Cooker: 6-quarts

Serving Size: 559 g   **Serves:** 10

Calories: 504

Total Fat: 33.6 g **Saturated Fat:** 14.3 g; **Trans Fat:** 0 g

Protein: 38 g

Total Carbs: 12 g; **Dietary Fibre:** 4.7 g; **Sugars:** 6.2 g

Net Carbs: 7.3 g

Cholesterol: 167 mg; **Sodium:** 2544 mg; **Potassium:** 792 mg

Vitamin A: 87%; **Vitamin C:** 10%; **Calcium:** 86%; **Iron:** 84%

Ingredients:
- ☐ 6 pounds corned beef
- ☐ 4 cups water
- ☐ 4 carrots, sliced
- ☐ 1/2 teaspoon salt
- ☐ 1/2 teaspoon ground thyme
- ☐ 1/2 teaspoon ground mustard
- ☐ 1/2 teaspoon ground marjoram
- ☐ 1/2 teaspoon ground coriander
- ☐ 1/2 teaspoon black pepper
- ☐ 1/2 teaspoon allspice
- ☐ 1 small onion, sliced
- ☐ 1 large head of cabbage, top layer removed, washed, quartered
- ☐ 1 celery bunch, sliced

Directions:
1. Line the carrots, onions, and celery into the bottom of the slow cooker.
2. Pour the 4 cups of water.
3. In a small mixing bowl, mix all of the spices together.

4. Rub both sides of the corned beef with the spices mixture and then place on top of the vegetables in the slow cooker.
5. Cover with the lid. Cook for 7 hours on low.
6. After 7 hours, place the cabbage in the slow cooker and cook for another 1 hour on low.

Beef Stroganoff

Prep Time: 20 minutes   **Cook Time:** Low for 8 hours

Slow Cooker: 3-quarts

Serving Size: 269 g   **Serves:** 4 (1 cup stroganoff over 1/2 cup zoodles)

Calories: 366

Total Fat: 19.5 g **Saturated Fat:** 10.1 g; **Trans Fat:** 0 g

Protein: 38.9 g

Total Carbs: 8.5 g; **Dietary Fibre:** 1.7 g; **Sugars:** 2.4 g

Net Carbs: 6.8 g

Cholesterol: 126 mg; **Sodium:** 490 mg; **Potassium:** 799 mg

Vitamin A: 11%; **Vitamin C:** 13%; **Calcium:** 9%; **Iron:** 130%

Ingredients:

- ☐ 1 piece (1 pound) top round steak (1 inch thick), trimmed
- ☐ 1 package (8 ounces or about 2 cups) mushrooms, sliced
- ☐ 1 cup chopped onion
- ☐ 1/2 teaspoon dried dill
- ☐ 1/2 teaspoon freshly ground black pepper
- ☐ 1/2 teaspoon salt
- ☐ 2 tablespoons Dijon mustard
- ☐ 2 tablespoons fresh parsley, chopped
- ☐ 3 garlic cloves, minced
- ☐ 1 container (8 ounces) sour cream

For the sauce:

- ☐ 1 1/2 ounces (about 1/3 cup) all-purpose flour
- ☐ 1 cup beef broth, low sodium

For serving:

- ☐ 2 cups spaghetti squash or zucchini pasta, hot cooked

Directions:

1. Across the grain, cut the steak diagonally into 1/4-inch thick slices. Place into the slow cooker. Except for the sour cream, add the rest of the ingredients into the slow cooker. Stir well.
2. In a small bowl, add the all-purpose flour. Then gradually add in the broth, stirring with a whisk until well blended. Add the broth mix into the slow cooker. Stir well.
3. Cover the slow cooker with lid. Cook for2 hour on high. Reduce the heat to low and cook for 7-8 hours or until the steak is cooked and tender. When cooked, remove the lid, turn off the slow cooker. Allow to stand for 10 minutes. Stir in the sour cream. Serve over spaghetti squash or zucchini pasta. If desired, garnish with fresh dill.

Beef Short Ribs Barbecue with Vegetables

Prep Time: 20 minutes **Cook Time:** Low for 6-8 hours	
Slow Cooker: 6-quarts	
Serving Size: 419 g **Serves:** 6	
Calories: 618	
Total Fat: 26.5 g **Saturated Fat:** 9.6 g; **Trans Fat:** 0 g	
Protein: 80.4 g	
Total Carbs: 12.5 g; **Dietary Fibre:** 2.3 g; **Sugars:** 7.8 g	
Net Carbs: 10.2 g	
Cholesterol: 241mg; **Sodium:** 1191 mg; **Potassium:** 1252 mg	
Vitamin A: 153%; **Vitamin C:** 14%; **Calcium:** 7%; **Iron:** 33%	

Ingredients:

- ☐ 3 1/2-pound beef short ribs
- ☐ 4 medium carrots, pared, cubed
- ☐ 1/2 cup tomato ketchup
- ☐ 1 cup water
- ☐ 1 large onion, cut into wedges
- ☐ 1 tablespoon cornstarch, optional
- ☐ 1 tablespoon paprika
- ☐ 1 tablespoon vegetable oil
- ☐ 1 teaspoon curry powder
- ☐ 1/2 teaspoon chili powder
- ☐ 1/2 teaspoon dry mustard
- ☐ 1/3 cup red wine vinegar
- ☐ 2 teaspoons salt

Directions:

1. Put all of the ingredients in the slow cooker. Stir to mix. Cover slow cooker with lid. Cook for 6-8 hours on low.

Curried Slow Pork Stew

Prep Time: 30 minutes	**Cook Time:** Low for 8 hours

Slow Cooker: 4-quarts

Serving Size: 235g   **Serves:** 6

Calories: 171

Total Fat: 6 g **Saturated Fat**: 1 g; **Trans Fat**: 0.1 g

Protein: 17 g

Total Carbs: 12.9 g; **Dietary Fibre:** 4.4 g; **Sugars:** 7.3 g

Net Carbs: 8.5 g

Cholesterol: 41 mg; **Sodium**: 210 mg; **Potassium**: 748 mg

Vitamin A: 4%; **Vitamin C**: 67%; **Calcium**: 7%; **Iron**: 10%

Ingredients:

- ☐ 1 cup (180 g) canned diced tomatoes
- ☐ 1 onion, sliced
- ☐ 1 pound (455 g) boneless pork loin, cubed
- ☐ 1 tablespoon (15 ml) canola oil
- ☐ 1/2 cup (120 ml) cider vinegar
- ☐ 1/2 teaspoon salt
- ☐ 2 cups (200 g) diced cauliflower
- ☐ 1 rutabaga, cubed
- ☐ 2 tablespoons (12 g) curry powder, divided
- ☐ 2 packets of Stevia

Directions:

1. Season the pork loin with salt. Sprinkle with 1 tablespoon of the curry powder.
2. In a large skillet, heat the canola oil over medium-high heat. Brown all the sides of the pork.
3. Put the turnips and the onion into the slow cooker. Place the browned pork over the turnip and onion layer. Add in the tomatoes.

4. In a mixing bowl, stir the vinegar, the remaining curry powder, and the stevia. Pour the mix over the pork. Cover the slow cooker with the lid. Cook for about 7 hours on low.

5. After 7 hours, stir in the cauliflower. Re-cover. Cook for another 1 hour on low until the cauliflower is tender.

Savory Slow Ham

Prep Time: 20 minutes   **Cook Time:** Low for 3-8 hours, plus 10 minutes

Slow Cooker: 3-4-quarts

Serving Size: 322 g   **Serves:** 6

Calories: 554

Total Fat: 22.7 g **Saturated Fat:** 8.3 g; **Trans Fat:** 0 g

Protein: 66 g

Total Carbs: 14.8 g; **Dietary Fibre:** 0 g; **Sugars:** 13.6 g

Net Carbs: 14.8 g

Cholesterol: 179 mg; **Sodium:** 274 mg; **Potassium:** 1103mg

Vitamin A: 0%; **Vitamin C:** 32%; **Calcium:** 5%; **Iron:** 15%

Ingredients:
- 1 sugar-free ham (about 2-3 pounds)
- 2 tablespoons honey
- 1/4 teaspoon ground cloves (or 4 whole cloves)
- 1/2 teaspoon black pepper
- 1/2 cup white wine
- 1/2 cup orange juice
- 1 teaspoon dry mustard
- 1 cup chicken broth

For the sauce:
- 2 tablespoons honey
- Salt and pepper to taste

Directions:
1. Put the ham in the cooker. If it does not fit, trim the edges off to fit and then add the trimmed edges into the cooker as well. If you are using the ham with a flat end, put the ham I the cooker with the flat-side down.
2. In a small saucepan over medium heat, warm the remaining ingredients for about 4 minutes or until the mustard is dissolved and the honey is melted. Pour over the ham in the cooker.
3. Cover and cook on low.

For boneless ham:
1. Cook the ham on low for 2 hours or until the internal temperature reaches 140F. Check after 1 1/2 hours and then every 30 minutes after that using an instant read thermometer.
2. This method also works with spiral-sliced hams, which are usually bone-in. Just be sure to read the temperature of the meat nearest to the bone. When desired temperature is reached, let the ham rest for about 10 minutes before slicing.

Bone-in hams:
1. Cook for about 6-8 hours on low until you can partially shred the meat with a fork.
2. When the ham is cooked to your preference, remove from the cooker, allow to rest for 10 minutes, and then slice. Save the bone for ham stock.

For the sauce:
1. Pour the ham's cooking liquid into a saucepan. Heat over medium-high heat. Stir the honey and cook for about 8 minutes until the liquid is reduced, dark, and strongly flavored.
2. Season with salt and pepper. Pour over the sliced ham. Serve.

Tangy Meatloaf with Mushroom Sour Cream Sauce

Prep Time: 20 minutes   **Cook Time:** Low for 8-9 hours

Slow Cooker: 6-quarts

Serving Size: 371 g   **Serves:** 8

Calories: 512

Total Fat: 28 g **Saturated Fat:** 13.8 g; **Trans Fat:** 0 g

Protein: 48.9 g

Total Carbs: 14.8 g; **Dietary Fibre:** 0.7 g; **Sugars:** 1.9 g

Net Carbs: 13.5 g

Cholesterol: 211 mg; **Sodium:** 855 mg; **Potassium:** 835mg

Vitamin A: 14%; **Vitamin C:** 9%; **Calcium:** 14%; **Iron:** 92%

Ingredients:

- ☐ 1 pound ground beef
- ☐ 1 pound ground pork
- ☐ 1 dash pepper
- ☐ 1 teaspoon dried dill weed
- ☐ 1/2 cup finely chopped celery
- ☐ 1/4 cup chopped onion
- ☐ 2 1/4 cup soft bread crumbs
- ☐ 2 eggs, beaten
- ☐ 2 tablespoons chopped pimento
- ☐ 3/4 teaspoon salt
- ☐ 8 ounces onion sour cream dip, separate 1/2 cup

For the mushroom-sour cream sauce:

- ☐ Remaining 1/2 cup onion sour cream dip
- ☐ 1 can cream of mushroom soup

Directions:

1. In a large mixing bowl, combine the 1/2 cup onion sour cream dip, the eggs, celery, breadcrumbs, dill weed, pimento, onion, salt, and pepper. Combine well. Add in the ground pork and beef. Combine well with the rest of the ingredients.
2. In the slow cooker, crisscross 2 strips of 15x2-inches foil across the bottom and the up sides. Place the meat mix over the foil strips. Lightly press to form a round loaf. Make sure the meat does not touch the sides of the pot.
3. Cover the slow cooker with lid. Cook for 8-9 hours on low.
4. Using the foil as handles, lift out the meat loaf. Drain the excess fat off.
5. In a saucepan, mix the mushroom-sour cream sauce ingredients together. Heat through, occasionally stirring. Serve with   the   meatloaf.

Classic Corned Beef and Cabbage

Prep Time: 25 minutes   **Cook Time:** Low for 8-9 hours

Slow Cooker: 4-6-quarts

Serving Size: 562 g   **Serves:** 6

Calories: 454

Total Fat: 28.5 g **Saturated Fat:** 12.2 g; **Trans Fat:** 0 g

Protein: 32.8 g

Total Carbs: 16.3 g; **Dietary Fibre:** 5.3 g; **Sugars:** 8.4 g

Net Carbs: 11 g

Cholesterol: 142 mg; **Sodium:** 2073 mg; **Potassium:** 781 mg

Vitamin A: 206%; **Vitamin C:** 83%; **Calcium:** 10%; **Iron:** 72%

Ingredients:
- 2-3 pounds corned beef brisket with seasoning packet
- 6 carrots, organic, cut into chunks
- 1 cabbage, organic, wedged
- 2 onions, organic, chopped
- 2-3 cups water

Directions:
1. Combine the cabbage, carrots, and onions in the cooker.
2. Rinse the corned beef under running cold water. Pat dry with paper towels. Put in the cooker. Sprinkle the seasoning mix over. Pour the water over the meat.
3. Cover and cook for about 8-9 hours on low.

To serve:
1. Across the meat grain, cut the corned beef into thin slices.
2. With a slotted spoon, remove the vegetables from the cooker. Serve with the corned beef. Pour the cooking liquid over. Serve with mustard on the side.

Notes:
If you are not serving immediately, remove the beef and the vegetables from the cooker. Cover with foil and keep warm in the oven at 100F.

Sweet Pork Roast

Prep Time: 30 minutes   **Cook Time:** Low for 8-9 hours

Slow Cooker: 4-quarts

Serving Size: 229 g   **Serves:** 2

Calories: 288

Total Fat: 11.9 g **Saturated Fat:** 2.9 g; **Trans Fat:** 0 g

Protein: 39 g

Total Carbs: 4 g; **Dietary Fibre:** 0 g; **Sugars:** 3 g

Net Carbs: 4 g

Cholesterol: 107 mg; **Sodium:** 282 mg; **Potassium:** 2941 mg

Vitamin A: 0%; **Vitamin C:** 4%; **Calcium:** 2%; **Iron:** 7%

Ingredients:

- ☐ 3 pounds pork loin, boneless
- ☐ 2 teaspoons dry mustard
- ☐ 2 tablespoons canola oil
- ☐ 1/4 cup soy sauce
- ☐ 1/2 cup chicken broth
- ☐ 1/2 cup (12 g) Splenda
- ☐ 1 can (8 ounces) tomato sauce

Optional:

Guar or xanthan

Directions:

1. In a large skillet, brown all sides of the pork in canola oil. Transfer the browned pork into the slow cooker.
2. In a mixing bowl, mix the soy sauce, tomato sauce, dry mustard, Splenda, and broth together. Pour the mix over the pork. Cover the slow cooker with the lid. Cook for 8-9 hours on low.

3. When the pork is cooked, transfer into a serving platter. If needed, thicken the cooking liquid with xanthan or guar. Serve the sauce with the pork.

New England Dinner

Prep Time: 30 minutes   **Cook Time:** Low for 10-12 hours plus high for 30 minutes

Slow Cooker: 6-quarts	
Serving Size: 329 g **Serves:** 8	
Calories: 281	
Total Fat: 10.2 g **Saturated Fat:** 2.8 g; **Trans Fat:** 0.6 g	
Protein: 38 g	
Total Carbs: 10.2 g; **Dietary Fibre:** 4 g; **Sugars:** 4 g	
Net Carbs: 6 g	
Cholesterol: 126mg; **Sodium:** 178 mg; **Potassium:** 1003 mg	
Vitamin A: 166%; **Vitamin C:** 65%; **Calcium:** 17%; **Iron:** 32%	

Ingredients:

- ☐ 3 pounds corned beef
- ☐ 6 small turnips, peeled and quartered
- ☐ 2 large stalks celery, cut into chunks
- ☐ 2 medium onions, cut into chunks
- ☐ 1/2 head cabbage, cut into wedges

For serving:

- ☐ Spicy brown mustard
- ☐ Horseradish
- ☐ Butter

Directions:

1. Put the turnips, celery, and the onions into the slow cooker. Put the corned beef over the vegetables. Pour in the water. If the corned beef has a seasoning packet, pour the contents into the slow cooker. Cover. Cook for about 10-12 hours on low.

2. After 10-12 hours, remove the corned beef from the slow cooker. Using tongs or a fork, transfer the corned beef into a serving platter. Cover with foil to keep warm.

3. Put the cabbage into the slow cooker with the remaining vegetables. Re-cover. Adjust heat to high and cook for 30 minutes.

4. Using a slotted spoon, remove the vegetables from the slow cooker. Pile them around the corned beef. Serve with butter as condiment for the vegetables together with horseradish and mustard as condiment for the beef.

Snacks

Balsamic Tomatoes

Prep Time: 10 minutes	**Cook Time:** Low for 2 hours; high for 1 hour

Slow Cooker: 3 or 3 1/2-quart

Serving Size: 163 g   **Serves:** 4

Calories: 392

Total Fat: 32.4 g **Saturated Fat:** 3.4 g; **Trans Fat:** 0 g

Protein: 15.2 g

Total Carbs: 13.6 g; **Dietary Fibre:** 6.6 g; **Sugars:** 4.2 g

Net Carbs: 7 g

Cholesterol: 5 mg; **Sodium:** 145 mg; **Potassium:** 541 mg

Vitamin A: 17%; **Vitamin C:** 22%; **Calcium:** 19%; **Iron:** 11%

Ingredients:
- ☐ 2 large (about 10 ounces each) tomatoes, under ripe, firm, halved crosswise
- ☐ 1 tablespoon balsamic vinegar
- ☐ 1 teaspoon dried basil, crushed
- ☐ 1/2 teaspoon dried oregano, crushed
- ☐ 1/4 teaspoon dried rosemary, crushed
- ☐ 1/8 teaspoon salt
- ☐ 2 garlic cloves, minced
- ☐ 2 teaspoons canola oil

For the Breadcrumb-Cheese Sprinkle:
- ☐ 3/4 cup almonds, roasted, crushed
- ☐ 2 tablespoons Parmesan cheese, grated

Optional:
- ☐ Fresh basil, snipped

For greasing the slow cooker:

- ☐ Canola oil or Nonstick cooking spray

Directions:

1. Lightly grease the slow cooker with canola oil or cooking spray. With the cut sides up, place the tomatoes in the bottom of the slow cooker.
2. In small bowl, combine the rest of the ingredients. Spoon evenly over the tomatoes.
3. Cover with lid. Cook for 2 hours on low or for 1 hour of high.
4. Meanwhile, cook the breadcrumb-cheese sprinkle. Heat a medium non-stick skillet over medium-high heat. Add in the breadcrumbs. Cook for about 2-3 minutes, stirring constantly, until the breadcrumbs are lightly brown. Remove from heat. Stir in the grated cheese.
5. Remove the cooked tomatoes from the slow cooker. Place on a serving platter. Evenly drizzle the cooking liquid over the tomatoes. Sprinkle with the breadcrumb-cheese mix. Let stand for 10 minutes. Garnish with fresh basil, if desired.

Lime and Rosemary Asparagus

Prep Time: 15 minutes	**Cook Time:** Low for 2hours
Slow Cooker: 3-quarts	
Serving Size: 118 g **Serves**: 4	
Calories: 25	
Total Fat: 0.2 g **Saturated Fat**: 0.1 g; **Trans Fat:** 0 g	
Protein: 3 g	
Total Carbs: 5 g; **Dietary Fibre:** 2 g; **Sugars:** 2 g	
Net Carbs: 3 g	
Cholesterol: 0 mg; **Sodium:** 2 mg; **Potassium:** 237 mg	
Vitamin A: 17%; **Vitamin C**: 14%; **Calcium**: 3%; **Iron**: 14%	

Ingredients:

- ☐ 1-pound asparagus spears, woody parts trimmed off
- ☐ 1 teaspoon dried rosemary
- ☐ 1 clove garlic, crushed
- ☐ 1 tablespoon lemon juice

Directions:

1. Put the asparagus into the slow cooker. If needed, cut the spears to fit.
2. Sprinkle with the rosemary and the garlic. Pour the lemon juice over.
3. Close the slow cooker lid. Cook for about 2 hours on low or until tender.

Fruit Chutney Chips

Prep Time: 20 minutes	**Cook Time:** High for 2 hours

Slow Cooker: 3 1/2or 4-quart

Serving Size: 74 g **Serves:** 24

Calories: 97

Total Fat: 2.1 g **Saturated Fat:** 1.2 g; **Trans Fat:** 0 g

Protein: 3.1 g

Total Carbs: 16.9g; **Dietary Fibre:** 2.5 g; **Sugars:** 6.1 g

Net Carbs: 14.4 g

Cholesterol: 5 mg; **Sodium:** 78 mg; **Potassium:** 63 mg

Vitamin A: 2%; **Vitamin C:** 6%; **Calcium:** 6%; **Iron:** 4%

Ingredients:

- ☐ 2 large apples core, cut into 1-inch slices
- ☐ 2 large pears core, cut into 1-inch slices
- ☐ 1 cup whole cranberries, frozen or fresh, thaw if frozen
- ☐ 1 sweet onion; chop
- ☐ 1 teaspoon ground cinnamon
- ☐ 1 teaspoon ground ginger
- ☐ 1/3 cup brown sugar, packed
- ☐ 1/4 cup balsamic vinegar
- ☐ 1/8 teaspoon salt
- ☐ 2 tablespoons cold water
- ☐ 1 tablespoon cornstarch

For topping:

- ☐ 4 ounces' goat cheese crumbled

For serving:

- ☐ 1 recipe Spiced Chips

Directions:

1. Except for the cold water and the cornstarch, combine the rest of the ingredients in the slow cooker.
2. Cover with lid. Cook for 1 hour on high.
3. In a small mixing bowl, combine the cold water and cornstarch. Stir into the slow cooker.
4. Cover with lid. Continue cooking for 1 more hour on high.
5. Serve warm or at room temperature with the spiced chips and top each serving with the crumbled goat cheese.

Awesome Cheese Sauce and Vegetable Dippers

Prep Time: 20 minutes   **Cook Time:** Low for 2 hours

Slow Cooker: 6-quarts

Serving Size: 67 g   **Serves:** 12

Calories: 208

Total Fat: 17.1 g **Saturated Fat:** 10.9 g; **Trans Fat:** 0 g

Protein: 10.5 g

Total Carbs: 1.7 g; **Dietary Fibre:** 0 g; **Sugars:** 0 g

Net Carbs: 1.7 g

Cholesterol: 49 mg; **Sodium:** 425 mg; **Potassium:** 95 mg

Vitamin A: 12%; **Vitamin C:** 0%; **Calcium:** 28%; **Iron:** 2%

Ingredients:

- ☐ 12 ounces provolone cheese, cubed
- ☐ 6 ounces cream cheese, cubed
- ☐ 4 ounces blue cheese, divided
- ☐ 1 clove garlic, crushed
- ☐ 1/2 cup heavy cream
- ☐ 1/2 cup dry white wine

Serve with:

- ☐ Asparagus, blanched
- ☐ Green pepper, cut into strips
- ☐ Artichoke hearts (canned), well-drained, cut into quarters
- ☐ Marinated mushrooms
- ☐ Or any of your favorite vegetables

Directions:

1. Put the crushed garlic cloves in the bottom of the slow cooker. Put the cubed cream cheese in, forming a layer. Put the provolone on top of the cream cheese layer. Add in half of the

blue cheese. Add in the cream cheese next, and then pour the wine over. Close the slow cooker lid. Cook for 2 hours on low.

2. After 2 hours, open the cooker lid. The cheese will be in a gloppy mess. Using an electric blender, process until smooth. Serve with vegetable dippers.

Mushroom in Garlic-Hoisin Sauce

Prep Time: 15 minutes   **Cook Time:** Low for 5-6 hours; high for 2 1/2-3 hours

Slow Cooker: 3 1/2 or 4-quart

Serving Size: 89 g   **Serves:** 10 (1/4 cup)

Calories: 45

Total Fat: 0.6 g **Saturated Fat:** 0 g; **Trans Fat:** 0 g

Protein: 2.7 g

Total Carbs: 8.4 g; **Dietary Fibre:** 1.1 g; **Sugars:** 4.7 g

Net Carbs: 7.3 g

Cholesterol: 0 mg; **Sodium:** 211 mg; **Potassium:** 239 mg

Vitamin A: 0%; **Vitamin C:** 4%; **Calcium:** 1%; **Iron:** 12%

Ingredients:

- ☐ 24 ounces' button mushrooms, whole fresh, trimmed
- ☐ 2 tablespoons minced garlic, bottled
- ☐ 1/4-1/2 teaspoon red pepper, crushed
- ☐ 1/4 cup water
- ☐ 1/2 cup hoisin sauce, bottled

Directions:

1. Except for the mushrooms, combine the rest of the ingredients in the slow cooker. Add in the mushrooms. Stir well to coat.
2. Cover with lid. Cook for 5-6 hours on low or for 2 1/2-3 hours on high.
3. When cooked, remove the mushrooms with a slotted spoon. Discard the cooking liquid. Serve the mushrooms

warm with decorative toothpicks.

Chocolatey Slow Cooked Cake

Prep Time: 20 minutes   **Cook Time:** Low for 2 1/2-3 hours

Slow Cooker: 6-quarts

Serving Size: 83 g   **Serves:** 10

Calories: 330

Total Fat: 28.6 g **Saturated Fat:** 12.9 g; **Trans Fat:** 0 g

Protein: 12.8 g

Total Carbs: 11.6 g; **Dietary Fibre:** 5.9 g; **Sugars:** 2.4 g

Net Carbs: 5.7 g

Cholesterol: 111 mg; **Sodium:** 167 mg; **Potassium:** 524mg

Vitamin A: 8%; **Vitamin C:** 2%; **Calcium:** 14%; **Iron:** 26%

Ingredients:

- ☐ 4 large eggs
- ☐ 3/4 cup sweetener of choice
- ☐ 3/4 cup almond or coconut milk, unsweetened
- ☐ 2/3 cup cocoa powder
- ☐ 2 teaspoons baking powder
- ☐ 1/4 teaspoon salt
- ☐ 1/4 cup whey protein powder, unflavored
- ☐ 1/2 cup butter, melted
- ☐ 1 teaspoon vanilla extract
- ☐ 1 1/2 cups almond flour

Optional:

- ☐ 1/2 cup chocolate chips, sugar-free

Directions:

1. Grease the slow cooker.
2. In a medium mixing bowl, whisk the almond flour, baking powder, cocoa powder, protein powder, sweetener, and salt together.

3. Stir in the milk, eggs, butter, and vanilla extract. Stir until well combined. Stir in the chocolate chips, if using.
4. Pour into the greased slow cooker. Cook for 2 1/2-3 hours on low. Turn off the slow cooker. Let cool for 20-30 minutes. When cooled to a warm, cut into slices. Serve lightly topped with whipped cream.

Pecan-Pumpkin Spice Cake

Prep Time: 30 minutes	**Cook Time:** Low for 2 1/2 -3 hours

Slow Cooker: 6-quarts

Serving Size: 67g **Serves**: 10

Calories: 134

Total Fat: 9.9 g **Saturated Fat:** 6.3 g; **Trans Fat:** 0 g

Protein: 7.2 g

Total Carbs: 5.1 g; **Dietary Fibre:** 1.7 g; **Sugars:** 1.7 g

Net Carbs: 3.4 g

Cholesterol: 98 mg; **Sodium**: 133mg; **Potassium**: 247 mg

Vitamin A: 81%; **Vitamin C**: 3%; **Calcium**: 8%; **Iron**: 12%

Ingredients:

- [ ] 4 large eggs
- [ ] 3/4 cup Swerve Sweetener
- [ ] 2 teaspoon baking powder
- [ ] 1/4 teaspoon salt
- [ ] 1/4 teaspoon ground cloves
- [ ] 1/4 cup whey protein powder, unflavored
- [ ] 1/4 cup butter, melted
- [ ] 1/3 cup coconut flour
- [ ] 1 teaspoon vanilla extract
- [ ] 1 teaspoon ground ginger
- [ ] 1 cup pumpkin puree
- [ ] 1 1/2 teaspoon ground cinnamon
- [ ] 1 1/2 cups raw pecans

Directions:

1. Grease the slow cooker or line with parchment paper.
2. Put the pecans in a high-powered blender. Process the pecans until ground into coarse meal. Make sure not to turn them into butter. Transfer into a large mixing bowl.

3. Into the bowl with pecan meal, whisk the coconut flour, baking powder, sweetener, protein powder, ginger, cloves, cinnamon, and salt.
4. Stir in the eggs, pumpkin puree, butter, and the vanilla. Stir until well combined.
5. Spread the mix into the greased slow cooker. Cook for 2 1/2 -3 hours on low or until set and the top is firm to the touch.

Rosemary Acorn Squash

Prep Time: 5 minutes	**Cook Time:** Low for 7-8 hours, high for 4 hours

Slow Cooker: 3-4-quarts

Serving Size: 156 g	**Serves:** 4

Calories: 122

Total Fat: 14 g **Saturated Fat:** 2.9 g; **Trans Fat:** 0 g

Protein: 11.1 g

Total Carbs: 4 g; **Dietary Fibre:** 0 g; **Sugars:** 3 g

Net Carbs: 4 g

Cholesterol: 0 mg; **Sodium:** 682 mg; **Potassium:** 442 mg

Vitamin A: 9%; **Vitamin C:** 8%; **Calcium:** 24%; **Iron:** 10%

Ingredients:

- ☐ 1 acorn squash (or more)
- ☐ 3 tablespoons rosemary leaves, fresh, chopped
- ☐ 3 garlic cloves
- ☐ 2 tablespoons extra-virgin canola oil
- ☐ 1/2 cup liquid (water vegetable broth, or dry white wine)
- ☐ 1 teaspoon kosher salt
- ☐ 1 teaspoon freshly ground pepper
- ☐ 1 tablespoon balsamic vinegar

Directions:

1. Cut the squash in half. With a spoon, scoop out the seeds and discard. Cut each squash half into 4 slices.
2. Pour the liquid into the cooker. With the skin side down, put the squash in the slow cooker.
3. Drizzle the canola oil and then the balsamic vinegar over the squash slices.
4. Sprinkle with salt and pepper and then with a garlic press, mince the garlic over the squash.
5. Finally, sprinkle with the rosemary.
6. Cover and cook.
7. Remove the squash and transfer to a serving plate. Drizzle the remaining liquid over the squash.

Notes:
The skin will be tender enough to eat, but if you don't like it, you can cut them out.

Celery Spicy Chicken Dip

Prep Time: 15 minutes   **Cook Time:** Low for 3-4 hours

Slow Cooker: 1 1/2-quarts

Serving Size: 83 g **Serves:** 10

Calories: 125

Total Fat: 9.3 g **Saturated Fat:** 5.1 g; **Trans Fat:** 0 g

Protein: 6.8 g

Total Carbs: 3.5 g; **Dietary Fibre:** 0.6 g; **Sugars:** 1.9 g

Net Carbs: 2.9 g

Cholesterol: 38mg; **Sodium:** 195 mg; **Potassium:** 161 mg

Vitamin A: 10%; **Vitamin C:** 3%; **Calcium:** 4%; **Iron:** 3%

Ingredients:

- ☐ 8 ounces cream cheese cut up
- ☐ 1/4-1/2 cup Buffalo wing sauce, bottled
- ☐ 1 stalk celery, finely chopped (about 1/2 cup)
- ☐ 1 fresh jalapeño chili pepper, seeded and minced
- ☐ 1 cup chicken breast, cooked and chopped
- ☐ 1 1/2 tablespoons blue cheese salad dressing, bottled, reduced-calorie

For serving:

- ☐ 20 stalks celery, halved crosswise

Directions:

1. Except for the celery stalks, put all of the ingredients together in the slow cooker.
2. Cover with lid. Cook for 3-4 hours on low. Serve with the celery.

Creamy Mushrooms and Green Beans

Prep Time: 20 minutes	**Cook Time:** Low for 4 hours
Slow Cooker: 4-quarts	
Serving Size: 154 g	**Serves:** 6
Calories: 176	
Total Fat: 13.8 g **Saturated Fat:** 8.6 g; **Trans Fat:** 0 g	
Protein: 7.2 g	
Total Carbs: 7.7 g; **Dietary Fibre:** 3 g; **Sugars:** 2 g	
Net Carbs: 4.7 g	
Cholesterol: 47mg; **Sodium:** 253 mg; **Potassium:** 271mg	
Vitamin A: 25%; **Vitamin C:** 44%; **Calcium:** 18%; **Iron:** 8%	

Ingredients:

- ☐ 4 ounces mushrooms, chopped
- ☐ 1/8 teaspoon pepper
- ☐ 1/4 medium onion, chopped
- ☐ 1/4 cup jarred roasted red pepper, diced
- ☐ 1 teaspoon beef bouillon granules
- ☐ 1 pound green beans (frozen), thawed
- ☐ 1 cup heavy cream
- ☐ 1 cup cheddar cheese, shredded
- ☐ 1 1/2 teaspoons spicy brown mustard

Directions:

1. Grease the slow cooker with cooking spray. Put in the green beans, mushrooms, onion, red peppers, and cheese. Stir to combine.
2. In a mixing bowl, combine the bouillon concentrate, cream, mustard, and pepper. Stir until the bouillon is dissolved. Pour the mix over the veggies.
3. Close the slow cooker lid. Cook for 4 hours on low. Stir and serve.

Hearts and Tuna Stuffed Mushrooms

Prep Time: 45 minutes	**Cook Time:** Low for 4-5 hours

Slow Cooker: 6-quarts
Serving Size: 128g **Serves:** 15
Calories: 142
Total Fat: 9 g **Saturated Fat:** 4.5 g; **Trans Fat:** 0 g
Protein: 10.7 g
Total Carbs: 6.2 g; **Dietary Fibre:** 2.2 g; **Sugars:** 1.8 g
Net Carbs: 4 g
Cholesterol: 29mg; **Sodium:** 197 mg; **Potassium:** 366 mg
Vitamin A: 7%; **Vitamin C:** 11%; **Calcium:** 10%; **Iron:** 13%

Ingredients:

- ☐ 8 ounces Italian cheese blend, shredded
- ☐ 3 tablespoons mayonnaise
- ☐ 3 scallions, sliced, include the crisp green shoot
- ☐ 3 ounces cream cheese, softened
- ☐ 2 pounds mushrooms, cleaned, stems removed
- ☐ 1/4 cup fresh parsley, minced
- ☐ 1/2 teaspoon pepper
- ☐ 1 can (7 ounces) tuna, in water, drained
     1 can (14 ounces) artichoke hearts, drained, chopped
- ☐ 1/4 teaspoon hot sauce

Directions:

1. In a large mixing bowl, put in the artichoke hearts, scallions, and the tuna. Mix until well combined. Then add in the Italian cheese, cream cheese, hot sauce, mayo, parsley and pepper. Use a fork to mash all the ingredients until well blended.

2. Stuff the tuna-artichoke mix into the mushroom caps.

3.   Place a basket-type steamer in the slow cooker. Arrange a layer of the stuffed mushrooms on the basket steamer.

4.   Take a piece aluminum foil. Make holes in the foil using a fork. Fit the holed aluminum foil down the first layer of the stuffed mushrooms. Make a hole in the middle. Arrange another layer of stuffed mushrooms on the foil. Repeat the process until all the mushrooms are arranged. Close the lid. Cook for about 4-5 hours on low. When cooked, serve in the slow cooker to keep warm or transfer them into a serving platter.

Sausage-Cauliflower Stuffed Peppers

Prep Time: 30 minutes	**Cook Time:** Low for 6 hours

Slow Cooker: 3-4-quarts

Serving Size: 184 g   **Serves:** 10 (1/2 pepper)

Calories: 210

Total Fat: 13.3 g **Saturated Fat:** 4.2 g; **Trans Fat:** 0.1 g

Protein: 11.6 g

Total Carbs: 11.9 g; **Dietary Fibre:** 3.7 g; **Sugars:** 6.7 g

Net Carbs: 8.2 g

Cholesterol: 38 mg; **Sodium:** 379 mg; **Potassium:** 655 mg

Vitamin A: 47%; **Vitamin C:** 173%; **Calcium:** 4%; **Iron:** 12%

Ingredients:
- ☐ 1 pound ground Italian hot sausage
- ☐ 5 assorted bell peppers, (2 red, 2 green, 1 yellow or any color combination of your choice)
- ☐ 2 teaspoons dried thyme
- ☐ 2 teaspoons dried oregano
- ☐ 1/2 head garlic, minced
- ☐ 1/2 head cauliflower, chopped or grated into "rice" consistency
- ☐ 1 small white onion, medium dice
- ☐ 1 small handful fresh basil, minced (or 2 teaspoons dried)
- ☐ 1 small can (8 ounces) tomato paste

Directions:
1. Cut the tops of the peppers off, saving them for later. Scoop out and then discard the seeds.
2. Chop or process about 1/2 of the cauliflower head into rice consistency. Put in a large mixing bowl.
3. Add the basil, garlic, onion, and the dried herbs in the bowl. Mix by hand.
4. Lightly brown the sausage in a very hot skillet. You can opt not to do this, but searing them enhances the flavor of the dish.

5. Add the seared sausage into the cauliflower mixture. Add the tomato paste. Mix by hand.
6. Fit as much of the sausage-cauliflower mixture into the peppers. Put the stuffed peppers into the cooker. Loosely place the pepper tops back on.
7. Cover and cook for about 6 hours on low.
8. When cooked, remove from the cooker. Carefully cut lengthwise to make 10 pepper halves.

Notes:
If you have extra stuffing, jam it between the peppers and cook together with the stuffed peppers. You can also save it for breakfast scramble.

Roasted Seeds and Nuts

Prep Time: 10 minutes	**Cook Time:** Low for 5-6 hours plus 45-60 minutes

Slow Cooker: 3-quarts

Serving Size: 44 g   **Serves:** 24 (1/3 cup)

Calories: 245

Total Fat: 21.8 g **Saturated Fat**: 3.9 g; **Trans Fat**: 0 g

Protein: 8.3 g

Total Carbs: 7.9 g; **Dietary Fibre:** 2.6 g; **Sugars:** 1.6 g

Net Carbs: 5.3 g

Cholesterol: 5 mg; **Sodium:** 197 mg; **Potassium:** 258 mg

Vitamin A: 2%; **Vitamin C:** 1%; **Calcium:** 3%; **Iron:** 16%

Ingredients:

- ☐ 4 tablespoons butter, melted
- ☐ 3 tablespoons Worcestershire sauce
- ☐ 2 teaspoons onion powder
- ☐ 2 cups raw pumpkin seeds, shelled
- ☐ 2 1/2 teaspoons seasoned salt
- ☐ 1 cup raw sunflower seeds, shelled
- ☐ 1 cup raw almonds
- ☐ 1 cup peanuts, dry-roasted
- ☐ 1 cup raw cashews
- ☐ 1 cup raw walnut pieces
- ☐ 1 cup raw pecans
- ☐ 1 1/2 teaspoons garlic powder

Directions:

1. Put the butter into the slow cooker. Turn the heat to low. Wait for the butter to melt.
2. Add in the Worcestershire sauce, onion powder, garlic powder, and the seasoned salt. Stir the ingredients to combine.

3. Add in the seeds and nuts. Stir to combine well and the seeds and nuts are evenly coated. Close the slow cooker lid. Cook for about 5-6 hours on low, stirring once or twice, if possible.

4. After 5-6 hours, uncover the pot. Stir the seeds and nuts. Cook for an additional 45-60 minutes or until they are dry. Allow to cool and store in an airtight container.

Beef Mushroom Sandwiches

Prep Time: 20 minutes	**Cook Time:** Low for about 7-8 hours

Slow Cooker: 3-4-quarts

Serving Size: 605 g   **Serves:** 3

Calories: 1425

Total Fat: 106.2 g **Saturated Fat:** 42 g; **Trans Fat:** 0 g

Protein: 105.0 g

Total Carbs: 8.2 g; **Dietary Fibre:** 2.6 g; **Sugars:** 3.5 g

Net Carbs: 5.6 g

Cholesterol: 389mg; **Sodium:** 760 mg; **Potassium:** 1448 mg

Vitamin A: 1%; **Vitamin C:** 10%; **Calcium:** 7%; **Iron:** 94%

Ingredients:

- ☐ 6 large portabella mushroom caps
- ☐ 2 1/2 pounds beef chuck roast, grass-fed
- ☐ 1 tablespoon red wine vinegar
- ☐ 1 teaspoon dried basil
- ☐ 1 teaspoon dried crushed rosemary
- ☐ 1 teaspoon dried oregano
- ☐ 1 teaspoon garlic powder
- ☐ 1 teaspoon onion powder
- ☐ 1/2 cup water
- ☐ 1/4 teaspoon black pepper
- ☐ 1/4-1/2 teaspoon salt
- ☐ 2 tablespoons Dijon mustard

Directions:

1. In a large skillet over medium-high heat, heat 1 tablespoon of oil.
2. Combine all the spices together and rub them on the roast.
3. Sear the roast in the skillet for about 4-5 minutes each side. Put in the cooker.
4. Add the water and the red wine vinegar.
5. Cook for about 7-8 minutes on low.
6. When cooked, remove the meat from the cooker and shred.

7. Skim any fat off the cooking juice in the cooker. Add the Dijon mustard. Stir to combine.
8. Return the shredded meat into the cooker. Mix.

For the mushroom buns:

1. Drizzle the mushrooms with oil. Season with salt and pepper. Roast at 450F for about 10 minutes. Sandwich shredded meat between 2 mushroom buns.

Notes:

You can also serve the meat with roasted carrots, zucchini, and cauliflower.

Indian Veggie Korma

Prep Time: 20 minutes	**Cook Time:** Low for 8 hours, high for 5 hours

Slow Cooker: 3-4-quarts

Serving Size: 211 g   **Serves:** 10

Calories: 134

Total Fat: 8.2 g **Saturated Fat:** 6.5 g; **Trans Fat:** 0 g

Protein: 4.7 g

Total Carbs: 14.1 g; **Dietary Fibre:** 6 g; **Sugars:** 6 g

Net Carbs: 8.1 g

Cholesterol: 0 mg; **Sodium:** 619 mg; **Potassium:** 619 mg

Vitamin A: 51%; **Vitamin C:** 117%; **Calcium:** 6%; **Iron:** 10%

Ingredients:
- ☐ 3/4 can coconut milk
- ☐ 2 tablespoons curry powder
- ☐ 2 tablespoons almond meal
- ☐ 2 large carrots, chopped
- ☐ 2 cloves garlic, minced
- ☐ 1/2 large onion, chopped
- ☐ 1/2 cup frozen green peas
- ☐ 1 teaspoon garam marsala
- ☐ 1 tablespoon sea salt
- ☐ 1 large cauliflower, broken into florets
- ☐ 1 cup green beans, chopped

Optional:
- ☐ 1 tablespoon red pepper flakes

Directions:
1. Put the cauliflower, green peas, carrots, green beans, garlic, and onion in the cooker. Mix well.
2. In a large mixing bowl, combine the curry powder, coconut milk, garam masala, sea salt, red pepper flakes. Mix well.
3. Pour the curry powder mixture evenly over the vegetables.
4. Sprinkle with the almond meal. Make sure the meal is well incorporated.

5. Cook until the mixture is very thick.
6. Serve immediately or allow to cool completely.

Storage:
Refrigerate for up to 1 week or freeze up to 2 months.

Chicken Liver and Mushrooms

Prep Time: 30 minutes	**Cook Time:** Low for 8 hours

Slow Cooker: 3-quarts

Serving Size: 87 g   **Serves:** 8

Calories: 160

Total Fat: 9.5 g **Saturated Fat:** 4.8 g; **Trans Fat:** 0.1 g

Protein: 14.4 g

Total Carbs: 42 g; **Dietary Fibre:** 0 g; **Sugars:** 0 g

Net Carbs: 2 g

Cholesterol: 336 mg; **Sodium:** 294 mg; **Potassium:** 200 mg

Vitamin A: 156%; **Vitamin C:** 29%; **Calcium:** 2%; **Iron:** 40%

Ingredients:

- [ ] 1 pound chicken livers, cut into halves
- [ ] 1 cup sliced mushrooms
- [ ] 3/4 teaspoon salt
- [ ] 3 tablespoons butter
- [ ] 2 tablespoons heavy cream
- [ ] 2 tablespoons brandy
- [ ] 1/2 teaspoon pepper
- [ ] 1/2 teaspoon dried thyme
- [ ] 1/2 teaspoon dried marjoram
- [ ] 1/2 cup onion, finely chopped
- [ ] 1 tablespoon fresh parsley, chopped
- [ ] 1 clove garlic, crushed
- [ ] 1 bay leaf, crumbled

Directions:

1. In a large skillet over low heat, sauté the garlic, onion, and the mushrooms in butter. When the mushrooms are soft, add in the chicken livers. Cook until the liver has changed color but not cooked through. Put the mix into a blender and process.

2. Add in the brandy, cream, thyme, bay leaf, parsley, marjoram, salt, and pepper. Process again until the mix is pureed finely.

3. Grease a 3 or 4-cup glass dish with cooking spray. Pour the pureed mix into the dish. Place the dish into the slow cooker. Carefully pour water around the dish until 1-inch blow the rim of the dish. Close the slow cooker lid. Cook for 8 hours on low.

4. After 8 hours, turn the heat off. Let the water cool. Remove the dish. Chill overnight before serving. Spread over a bed of greens.

Conclusion

Thank you again for downloading this book. I hope that the recipes help you stay on the Ketogenic Diet!

Finally, if you enjoyed this book, I'd like to ask you to leave a review for my book on Amazon. It would be greatly appreciated!

I am constantly looking for ways to improve my content to give readers the best value. So, if you didn't like the book, I would like to also hear from you:

Twitter: @JeremyStoneEat

Email: Elevatecan@gmail.com

Thank you and good luck!

You might also be interested in...

Are you too busy to cook every day but still want to eat healthy Ketogenic recipes?

We all know that Ketogenic eating is hard and cooking healthy food every day is even harder! Meal prepping has taken off in popularity because it can solve both issues at once. By making large healthy meals in one setting, you can have nutritious Ketogenic meals throughout the week without having to waste time cooking and cleaning every day!

This book is designed to empower you by providing essential meal prepping techniques along with tasty Ketogenic recipes to help you make healthy meals that last you throughout the week. With The Essential Ketogenic Meal Prep Guide you get ...

- Over 50 Ketogenic Meal Prep Recipes For All Meals – Breakfast, Lunch, Dinner, and Snacks!

- Full Nutritional Information For Each Recipe, Cooking And Preparation Times To Find The Quickest And Easiest Recipes To Make

- Essential Meal Prepping Techniques

- Suggested Ingredients To Include, Foods To Avoid

- Advice On Food Storage

- Meal Prep Hacks

To get these delicious recipes and more visit http://www.shortcuttoketosis.com/KetogenicMealPrep

Are you looking for healthy ketogenic snacks that will help you lose weight and taste great?

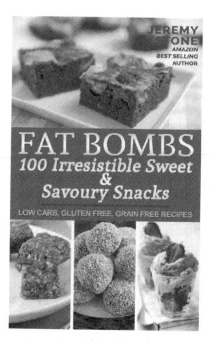

Trying to be healthy is hard and sometimes confusing. For years we were told that fats were bad for us and we had to cut them out of our diets. Yet we became more obese than any other time in history! But over time, science and our understanding of nutrition has improved. We now know that many fats are actually healthy for us. That's why fat bombs are the perfect snack when on a Keto Diet! This book is designed to empower you by providing delicious easy to make low carb fat bomb recipes.

With Fat Bombs: 100 Irresistible Sweet and Savoury Snacks you get ...

- ◆ Over 100 Ketogenic Recipes For Dessert Bars, Fudge, Candies, Pudding, Cookies, Cakes, Smoothies and More!

- Full Macro and Micro Nutritional Information For Each Recipe

- Easy to Follow Step-by-Step Instructions

To get these delicious recipes and more check out: http://www.shortcuttoketosis.com/FatBombs